The Art of Coexistence

How You and I Can Save the World

ILCHI LEE

WITH STEVE KIM

BEST
LIFE
MEDIA

BEST
LIFE
MEDIA

459 N. Gilbert Rd, A-275
Gilbert, AZ 85234
www.BestLifeMedia.com
480-926-2480

First paperback edition: April 2023
Library of Congress Control Number: 2023931087
ISBN-13: 978-1-947502-24-6

Cover and interior design by Kiryl Lysenka
Photo on page 5 © iStockPhoto.com/Peter Schaefer

*To the bright, benevolent minds that find joy
in seeking the truth and helping others.*

CONTENTS

Betting on Humanity

Whether within an individual lifespan or throughout the world's history, there will never be a time without conflict or challenge. But now, the scale and impact of our challenges have become incomparably broader and more significant than ever before. There are so many occurring at once—climate change, the threat of nuclear war, the breakdown of ecosystems, new technologies that might be difficult to control—that there isn't enough space to list them all.

The perception or response to the seriousness of these problems depends on the individual or group. Sometimes, our reactions are polarized to the point where reconciliation seems impossible. And this is happening everywhere in the world, not only in a few specific regions or countries. Seeing this situation raises the question: If we want to work together to overcome these challenges and create a better world, where would we have to start, and would there be a common foundation that applies to everyone?

This book is a response to this question. Its title, *The Art of Coexistence*, encapsulates that response. It is up to all of us whether this response will be the solution. Creating a world that's sustainable, peaceful, and realizes well-being for everyone is a goal that many people want and hope for, but what we need to achieve such a goal is neither a deep philosophy nor advanced technology nor overwhelming military power, but a demonstration of togetherness in the same time and space—to know how to coexist peacefully. In a way, coexistence is a natural principle that only makes sense. It's something we start learning from kindergarten, but unfortunately, we have yet to master these basics.

We can have hope, however, because the human mind and brain are already equipped with the abilities that make coexistence possible. Those abilities are introspection, conscience, and empathy. With them, we know how to reflect on ourselves, distinguish between right and wrong, feel uncomfortable about what is not right, and feel the pain of others. The beginning and foundation of this book is the belief that the brain—although it may sometimes lose its balance and fail to function—inherently has the ability to recover introspection, conscience, and empathy, so that anyone can naturally choose coexistence.

Ilchi Lee, the principal author of this book, has consistently carried out writing and educational endeavors with this belief throughout his life. Holding the root of his spiritual lineage in *Hongik* (to widely benefit all), the founding philosophy of the Korean people, he's shared his thoughts and insights in various forms such as Brain Education and the Earth Citizen Movement. At their core, however, his teachings come from his faith in the essential goodness in human nature.

Struck by Sincerity

I met Ilchi Lee 25 years ago in South Korea in my early thirties. It was at a time when I was experiencing intense inner turmoil from the conflict between yearning for a better world and not being able to make any meaningful changes. I felt through my meeting with him that his belief in essential human nature and his will to create a better world by helping restore that nature were simple, clear, and sincere. That simple and clear sincerity blew away the conflict in my mind. I chose to take him as my lifelong teacher. Afterward, I moved to the United States, and I've been helping him convey his heart ever since.

These past 25 years in the United States have been full of various challenges that led to successes and failures, big and small. However, as a result, the most important thing that remains is that the sincerity I originally witnessed is becoming my own more and more. I think it's the greatest gift I've ever received from Ilchi Lee and the best way I can repay it. The process of writing this book as a co-author has been a process of feeling and confirming it once again.

It is a great honor for me that I came to write this book with Ilchi Lee. And I am deeply grateful to him for giving me this opportunity. I hope that I helped the message of coexistence reach many more people.

Steve Kim

To My Fellow Earth Citizens

In the summer of 2022, after completing my work in New Zealand, South Korea, and Japan, I came back to the United States for the first time in a long while. At that time, I returned to Lake Powell in Northern Arizona, one of the places I used to often visit in the summer when I'm in the US. This is a very special place for me. Every time I go there, I receive new energy and inspiration for the future.

I'll never forget how deeply moved I was when I first visited Lake Powell in 1998. The jade-colored waters cutting across the desert and the magnificent rock formations surrounding the lake gave me the impression of a massive, ancient city. Traveling inside the canyon walls by boat for a couple of hours, I arrived at a great rock bridge, standing tall in a half-circle near the shore of the lake. This is called Rainbow Bridge—the second-largest natural bridge in the world, and a sacred place for the Navajo people. It is said they came here seeking wisdom and protection from Mother Nature, and that in years of drought they performed rain dances here. Likewise, I felt as though I could communicate directly with the earth in this special place.

Lake Powell and Rainbow Bridge show different aspects of the earth than what we typically encounter. Whenever I visit, I feel two conflicting sentiments. One is a sense of mystery and reverence, a feeling that I have merged with the body of Mother Earth. The other is a sense of the *mental state* of the earth, who mourns the life being destroyed by humans, and who worries about the future of humanity. Lake Powell and Rainbow Bridge deeply inscribed in my own mind a sense of gratitude and contrition that has become one of the important reasons I started the Earth Citizen Movement.

When I visited Lake Powell after an 11-year absence, the place had become completely different. Even at the time of my previous visits, the water level had been dropping contin-uously due to drought, but what I now saw was so shocking that my heart sank. The water level had fallen to 24 percent of its capacity—the lowest in the lake's history. Just a few years ago, it was possible to travel by boat to a dock not far from Rainbow Bridge. But now, visitors must hike more than three miles to reach Rainbow Bridge from the nearest place where a boat can be docked. The lake has become parched and barren, drained of life. If the drought continues, experts say, the lake might disappear entirely within a few decades.

I already knew that climate change had caused extreme droughts and floods in many parts of the world, and fresh-water sources are rapidly decreasing as a result. But seeing this spot that I had cherished so deeply now losing its mystery and beauty and succumbing to swift destruction, I felt an indescribable pain. Anguish bore into my heart.

Climate change and environmental destruction, which we are all experiencing more acutely than ever, are certainly the biggest global crises we currently face. However, they are not fundamental problems. There's a foundational issue that has brought about these problems and all other seemingly unrelated crises, crises such as the pandemic that's rocked the world since the end of 2019 and forced us to accept a completely new "normal"; the hegemonic competition between the United States and China; the war in Ukraine costing countless innocent lives; the persecution and oppression inflicted in the name of religion and ideology and the resistance that arose in response. Beneath all these challenges, I see the same root cause, a misperception that is driving our lives and the earth toward a catastrophic end.

The underlying problem lies neither in societal systems nor in the environment. Nor is it a matter of believing in the right supernatural being. The problem lies right here in our own selves. It's always easy to blame something outside of ourselves, but no change can happen until we reexamine who we really are, what we value most, and what kind of relationships we're building within our personal, social, and natural environments. Therefore, the starting point for solving these problems is found *within* ourselves.

I believe that the key to solving the global problems we've come up against lies in the meaning of this word: *coexistence*, or *gongsaeng* in Korean. Coexistence starts with the understanding that all life is interconnected and that if we fail to take care of each other, ultimately no individual can survive. Coexistence is not a new concept. What needs to change is the scope of it.

Until now, we have limited the scope of coexistence to "my family, my workplace, my country, and the communities to which I belong." But the current circumstances of the earth are urgently calling on us to extend that scope to *all* people, *all* life, and the planet itself. Fortunately, coexistence doesn't have to be difficult to learn; it is a sense and an ability inherent in all of us. Therefore, I believe that by choosing coexistence and awakening and utilizing our sense of coexistence, ordinary people like you and me can save the world. Coexistence is no longer one of many ways of life from which we can choose. It's the *only* way we can sustain life on this earth.

About This Book

About 20 years ago, I launched the Earth Citizen Movement. This was inspired by my belief that we are Earth Citizens before we are Koreans, Americans, or Indians, and before we are Christians, Buddhists, or Muslims. Through awakening to this realization, I am certain humanity can make a better world. Over the years, countless people from different backgrounds and cultures all over the world have joined the movement. I have written *The Art of Coexistence* together with Steve Kim, but in a sense this book is also a reflection of the experiences and learning of the many people who have taken part in the Earth Citizen Movement.

This book is an invitation that I'm sending out to my fellow Earth Citizens, to anyone who is truly concerned about the future of the earth and humankind. It's an invitation to participate in a conversation about what constitutes the root of the global crisis that we're all experiencing at present, and about how we can provide one another and the earth with strength and support in this interconnected world, instead of being a dangerous threat.

The Art of Coexistence consists of three sections. The key term for **Part 1** is the *sense* of coexistence. Within the great cycle of life, we all rely on each other to live. Coexistence is not an exception to a rule, attained only through hard learning and effort. Everywhere that life exists, coexistence is the most universal way of being. So what makes us distant from the sense of harmony and balance that nature has given to all life? What makes us ceaselessly destructive? To recover the sense of coexistence that we've lost, what must we look to and rely upon? The main point made in Part 1 is that we must find the answer in our own minds, rather than from an external source.

Part 2 addresses the topic of coexistence with the earth. How can we use our understanding of the earth's current problems to transform our modern lifestyle? How can we achieve harmony and cooperation between individuals and groups of differing interests, goals, and backgrounds? The key ideas of Part 2 include earth sensibility, which involves feeling that you yourself are connected with the earth, and earth management, which shifts your choices and value judgments from self-centered to earth-centric.

Part 3 proposes a plan for a society based on coexistence. It presents a different approach to education: prioritizing soft skills for living well together rather than competitive academic study and scores, planning out longevity personally and collectively for a more fulfilling life, forging a healthy relationship with technology, and ideas for true welfare. When we make coexistence and the earth itself the top priorities and apply that to society, what kind of changes can we make? What, specifically, can you and I do to bring about such changes? Part 3 presents new possibilities and alternatives to answer these questions, which I hope will fill you with high expectations and hope.

The Special Times We're Living In

We are living in a very special time. We are enveloped in layers of problems, any one of which could drive humankind to a catastrophic end. The pandemic, climate change, modern warfare, artificial intelligence, and so on—each of these is potentially bigger than any challenge humankind has ever experienced before. What these problems have in common is that they cannot be solved by any particular individual or group; they can only be solved when we all gather our strength together in solidarity.

Solutions to these problems cannot be found in new technologies or in greater resources. Though there are several serious problems, there is just one solution for solving it, and it's simple: each individual must have a bone-deep realization that "I myself, other people, and the earth are an inseparable oneness."

We are the first generation in human history that can change the world through personal choice. Until now, the power of individual choice has not been strong enough to change the condition of planet Earth. But now, humanity has unprecedented power to affect the earth and its ecosystems, and thus, our personal choices have come to have real significance.

Earth scientists say that the question, "Can we pass down a healthy Earth to future generations?" has passed its expiration date. We are in a crisis so dire that we need to be asking, "Are we going to be able to survive on Earth in a few decades?" Not only will the choices we make now certainly affect our descendants, but they are bound to determine our own survival as well. Simply being on Earth at this particular time puts us in a special position. And so there's a different level of introspection, wisdom, courage, and responsibility demanded of us compared to the generations that lived on the earth before us.

We are faced with many profound problems. But just as we fought our way through the challenge of an unprecedented worldwide pandemic, I believe we can face these other problems, too. The experience of the pandemic was painful, but at the same time, it showed us new possibilities and ways of generating hope. Wasn't it amazing how humanity adapted to the pandemic situation? In response, we quickly created new standards, systems, and cultures, and, while many lives were lost, many more lives were saved thanks to human ingenuity and cooperation.

Within each of us, there is a heart that loves human beings and the earth and wants everyone to be happy. There is an instinct to trust ourselves and our fellow human beings. Even if we don't have a perfect solution to all the challenges we face now, our hearts and our minds, and our faith, will find the answer in the end.

At this unique moment in history—which feels frightening, as though the foundation of our lives is about to be shattered—the minds of countless people are waking up. Many are looking back on their lives as they seek solutions, and they are making up their minds to do whatever it takes for the earth and humankind. I believe that you are one of those people. This book is an attempt to find Earth Citizens like you and me and to connect our hearts together so that we can lend inspiration and strength to one another.

Ilchi Lee

PART 1

Coexistence Is the Only Way

CHAPTER 1

Seeing the World through the Eyes of Coexistence

"The only alternative to coexistence is co-destruction."

— Jawaharlal Nehru

The clownfish is a cute little guy with a white band around its orange body. Thanks to his lovable appearance, he starred in a Pixar animated film, *Finding Nemo*. When a bigger fish attacks, looking for a meal, the clownfish hides in the sea anemone's tentacles. Hungry and oblivious, the bulkier fish pounces, only to be stung by the poisonous tentacles of the sea anemone, becoming a meal itself. Oddly enough, the venom in those tentacles is entirely harmless for the clownfish. The clownfish helps its protector, removing diseased tentacles from the sea anemone and cleaning up the debris.

In nature, it's not difficult to recognize symbiotic relationships like these, in which different species, such as clownfish and sea anemones, closely interact, living together without destroying one another. Many of us learned about this in elementary school. You may remember memorizing the names of creatures that exist in symbiotic relationships, like crocodiles and crocodile birds (Egyptian plovers), ants and aphids, and titmice and camellias.

Such well-known examples of symbiosis are actually part of a much broader network of coexistence. The natural world is full of organisms that coexist in similar relationships, including bees and flowers. Bees obtain honey and pollen from flowers; flowers bear fruit with the help of bees. This mutually beneficial coexistence profoundly affects the lives of other plants and animals as well. Most of the fruits and produce we eat would disappear without the coexistence of these two species.

A Broader Coexistence

In biology, we also learned about "natural enemies," a concept that's the opposite of symbiotic relationships. These are relationships connected by the food chain, with one side eating the other: small insects are eaten by flies, flies by frogs, and frogs by snakes. But are the links between such natural enemies lopsided—relationships in which one side merely destroys the other?

Originally derived from herring fishing, the "catfish effect" is a term also used in business administration. In the 17th and 18th centuries, herring was the primary source of income for the fishing communities of northern Europe. Because herring was caught in cold waters far from the mainland, many died during transportation. One Norwegian fisherman, though, made a fortune by bringing almost every herring to port still alive. This fisherman's secret—learned only after his death—was to put a few of the herrings' natural enemy, the catfish, in the tank with them. Feeling the threat of being eaten by the catfish, the herrings made it to port alive and fresh thanks to their efforts to flee in all directions. The very existence of their natural enemy increased their survivability.

Many examples in nature, like that of the catfish and herring, show that natural enemies aren't necessarily simply enemies. The relationship between lions and antelopes is typical of this. One might think the disappearance of a top predator such as a lion would result in a paradise for its herbivore prey, but that's not the case. Without lions, the antelope population increases too much, destroying grassland and ultimately creating an environment that's untenable even for antelopes.

The same goes for grasses and herbivores. Grasses should thrive without herbivores feeding on them, right? Wrong. The opposite is true. Herbivores cut the grass down appropriately, enabling new sprouts to get enough sunlight. The activities of these animals serve to cut, seed, and fertilize the grass. Without an adequate number of herbivores, the grass would grow tall and fall over, covering the ground and blocking sunlight. Seeds would be unable to put down proper roots, making growth difficult for future generations of the plant. Later the grass would disappear, resulting in progressing desertification.

In the natural world, many organisms seem hostile to each other—battling, eating, and being eaten by one another. However, viewing these species from a broader, long-term perspective reveals their interconnection, their mutual assistance being absolutely essential to both species. But, unfortunately, this great circle of life is invisible to eyes blinded by immediate gains. Seeing the massive circle of life connecting all living things requires eyes that see deep and far.

Meditating on a Cup of Water

Biological symbiosis is only a tiny part of the whole picture of coexistence. From a broader perspective, all living things are linked—giving and getting help—in the great circle of life. On a larger scale, this universal coexistence is part of a flow of energy and a cycling of matter that encompasses the entire planet.

In front of me right now is a glass of water. The liquid in this glass appears to be confined, separated from the rest of the world in a small space. That's why I can drink the water in front of me without much worry, even though I know that elsewhere water supplies are running dry or becoming dangerously polluted. I can even drink my water while watching a news story about polluted drinking water in yet another city. But, if I think that our planet's water problems are not my problem because I have a clean glass of water in front of me, I am deluded. My clean glass of water and the dirty, polluted water all come from the same source and the same system.

Nothing else travels the world as thoroughly and widely as water does. It floats with the wind in the form of clouds before falling to the ground as raindrops when conditions are right. Raindrops gather into streams that flow into rivers, creating a network that eventually reaches the sea.

As the rainwater makes its way to the ocean, the sun's rays beat down on the earth, causing evaporation, returning water from the land and sea to the clouds. The water in this cup that I hold is part of that cycle. A few hours after I drink it, any water that is not needed by my cells leaves my body, rejoining the flow. The cup in front of me and the inside of my body are no more than rest stops on that flow, places to take a break before moving on. The same molecules of water will cycle round and round in the system before returning to me one day.

We all exist as parts of the cycle and the energy flow of life, and we depend on one another to live. Coexistence is not a special case found in ecosystems of diverse life forms, or one of many approaches to living. It is the *only* way we can sustain life for long.

Why Humans Are Special

In the natural world, the cycle of life and the flow of energy occur spontaneously. There is no need for someone to intervene consciously. And water and air aren't alone in flowing spontaneously. Plant and animal ecosystems also take care of themselves. The lion, for example, instinctively hunts the antelope to satisfy its hunger. While it's chasing the antelope, the lion doesn't take pride in also helping to manage the antelope population. The antelope instinctively runs away to avoid being eaten. As it runs, the antelope never thinks that the lion is also performing the noble job of maintaining the balance of the savanna; from the antelope's perspective, the lion is a ruthless predator seeking to kill and devour it. Amid the hunting and fleeing, however, a cycle benefiting everyone is created and balance is maintained.

In nature, coexistence occurs spontaneously, without each animal or plant intentionally trying to coexist. So what makes humans different in their relationship with nature? Why can't people just take what we need from nature, like lions? Why don't the balance and harmony that occur spontaneously in nature apply to humans? Why are people special?

The most important reason is this: compared to other species, the impact of humans on nature is overwhelmingly greater than nature's ability to balance itself. The sum of human effects is already greater than any natural force, even if everyone is "good," living without causing much trouble. We know all too well what the consequences will be if humans mistakenly or intentionally use their powers to wreak havoc.

In the long history of evolution on Earth—more than four and a half billion years—no species is comparable to humanity in terms of influence. Even the dinosaurs, which dominated Earth's ecosystem for 150 million years, cannot be compared in influence to humans. The earliest record of Homo is 2.8 million years old, and the current human species, *Homo sapiens*, emerged in Africa only 300,000 years ago, but it has power over the whole planet beyond what any other life form has ever attained.

Why have humans become so influential? Population is one part of the explanation. Usually, species populations are lower when higher on the food chain. For example, when the ecosystem is in balance, the number of wolves at Yellowstone is much lower than the number of animals they hunt, such as deer and antelope. Additionally, different species typically compete with each other at the same chain level, maintaining balance. But at the top of the food chain, human numbers are overwhelmingly large, in contrast to other top predators.

As an example, only about 5,000 tigers are living in the wild. Lions are a little better off, but only 20,000 to 30,000 survive. In comparison, there are now about eight billion people on Earth. Even if we don't consider other conditions—such as human intelligence or technology— the fact that humanity is at the top of the food chain and has such a vast population puts the entire ecosystem in severe imbalance.

Paradoxically, humanity's success as a species demon- strates the tremendous flexibility, adaptability, and resilience of Earth's ecosystem. But, this precarious balancing act will be impossible to maintain if humanity continues its current trajectory. Just as a coiled spring loses its ability to bounce back if you pull it too far, nature will not be able to cope with the stresses humans impose on it.

Because we have the ability to disrupt the environment as we do, our behavior must become different from other species. If we take from our environment as much as we need or want, according to the instincts granted us by nature—like the lions hunting antelopes—eventually we won't be able to survive because nature cannot bear such exploitation over time. On top of that, we are an incred- ibly competitive species with all our knowledge, skills, and technologies. All these conditions make it clear that humans cannot simply follow our instinctive drive to take what we need without concern for the whole. Unfortunately, though, this is the way we've lived here on earth. And now, shocked by the scale of destruction this brings, we're struggling to find ways to undo our mistakes.

In nature, no plants or animals try to live harmoniously, thinking of coexistence. Each simply does its best to survive and reproduce under the conditions it has been given. Balance is achieved and harmony is created in such circumstances. But that same natural harmony doesn't apply to humans, a species that has moved far beyond such a position.

If humanity does as it wills, hoping that coexistence will happen on its own and leaving it for nature to work out, the end result will be self and mutual destruction. Our species has already passed the point in its relationship with nature where we can leave responsibility for coexistence to chance. Coexistence is a phenomenon in nature, but for humans, it is a choice and creation. There will be no coexistence in the future of the earth unless humans deliberately create it.

Unlike other life forms, humans have special abilities that enable such creativity. We have the ability to self-reflect, to choose and regulate our actions. We know that other animals also have intelligence. In particular, whales, dogs, gorillas, and chimpanzees are highly intelligent and capable of learning. Many maintain hierarchical order and show a simple division of labor and cooperation. But none of these species self-reflect, choose their actions, or go beyond themselves the way humans do, thinking of their relationship with their environment or other species. Even whales, known for their altruistic behavior in helping other animals who are in danger, wouldn't worry about polar bears or Siberian tigers just because they face the same extinction crisis. Only humanity can transcend the group to which it belongs to think of its environment and other life forms.

At present, no organism can correct the current imbalance on Earth unless we do so ourselves. If balance is restored without us, it will be because of the resilience of the earth itself. This will mean extinction or painful change close to that, not only for humankind but also for countless plants and animals existing along with us. Human behavior now brings fear, danger, and despair to other organisms. But despite this, humanity is the only species that other species can depend on for hope and change. In this sense, humankind is the only hope, not only for ourselves. We are simultaneously the source of despair and the one and only hope for all plant and animal life.

The Saving-the-Earth Delusion

When we talk about the earth's current environmental and ecological crisis, we often use the expression "saving the planet," and we actually think that's what we're doing. Of course, as in this book's subtitle, we can use such an expression for rhetorical reasons or emotional appeal. Strictly speaking, though, saving the planet is a delusion.

Earth has seen five mass extinctions in which more than two-thirds of all life forms have disappeared and been replaced by other species. Several times it has experienced climate change far more extreme than what's happening today. In this history of evolution, countless species have lasted longer than humans have. Some species, often referred to as living fossils, such as sharks, bracken, and cockroaches, have been inhabiting the planet far longer than we have. Our time here has been only one-fiftieth that of the dinosaurs who preceded us, ruling as the top predators of Earth's ecosystem.

What has remained as various life forms have changed is the planet itself. Biological species have been replaced in different ways, like actors on a stage, with characters coming and going as one act ends and the next begins. But the stage itself—Earth—has always been there, providing a foundation for all living things to express their individuality and to fill various roles.

We are the ones really facing a crisis right now. We can't predict how the earth will change if the present environmental crisis continues, and how to survive in a completely changed environment is probably no longer what we need to be concerned about. The fact is, if we don't do anything, the planet will find balance itself—as it's already done several times in its history. Such changes are already happening. The climate crisis is a part of that transition.

The restoration of Earth's balance, if we allow it to happen without our involvement, is likely to take a form completely different from what we want, however. And no one can say precisely how much time we have left. Even the forecasts of scientists vary widely, but a common prediction is that the current precarious balance won't last long.

Cities full of tall buildings made of steel, concrete, and glass; military forces capable of destroying every city on the planet; an information and communications system that can connect and monitor every corner of the globe—these all give the impression that the world is solid and sturdy. But reality has been very different. Through pandemics and trade disputes, typhoons and hurricanes, changes in monetary policies and wars, we have experienced and witnessed the fragility of our lives on a personal level and as a society.

With our current high level of dependence and low level of resilience, how long will we be able to withstand massive changes that we cannot control, predict, or even just anticipate? With our current status, if the planet itself triggers changes on the scale of past mass extinctions in order to restore balance, most of us probably won't be in the picture unfolding on Earth after those changes.

The Changes We Really Need

The signs and consequences of climate change and human-induced environmental destruction are already far too numerous. By searching the Internet, anyone can find out how many organisms vanish in a year, how many acres of forests are destroyed, and how many freshwater lakes disappear. The same goes for how much land turns into desert, how much garbage is dumped, and how much greenhouse gas is emitted. Plenty of photos and audio-visual materials are available to illustrate what's happening.

But simply presenting such data in greater detail and giving shocking examples won't bring about change. The problem is not a lack of information. The problem is changing our minds.

Most of us look at climate change and sustainability from a macroscopic perspective. We believe that developing new technologies, improving infrastructure, making international agreements, and passing new legislation could solve the problem. Since these are big issues beyond the reach of ordinary individuals, we think the experts, or representatives of governments and mega corporations—in other words, "somebody else"—will deal with them.

We live in a carbon-based civilization in which most of our energy production depends on fossil fuels and most of our production and consumption activities emit carbon dioxide. For example, currently, most transportation relies on petroleum-based internal combustion engines. A typical passenger vehicle emits about 404 grams of carbon dioxide while traveling one mile. Over a year, that adds up to be about 4.6 metric tons of carbon dioxide added to the atmosphere. While electric vehicles are becoming widely available, it will take at least 20 to 30 years for most to make the switch.

In the current state, trying to reduce carbon emissions without changing our consciousness or lifestyle ultimately means a reduction in economic activity. But what political leader could present negative economic growth as a vision? What company's CEO could choose reducing production, sales, and profits as a management goal? How many presidential candidates or corporate leaders would prioritize the earth at the risk of losing votes or having diminished returns? Unfortunately, this is the realistic position of the "someone else" we hope and expect will do something for us. Can we really hold someone else accountable, blaming them for not making the hard choices the earth needs?

While we wait for someone else to do the hard work for us, our lives grow more devastated, and the earth moves ever closer to the point of no return. But the changes we really need aren't information, technological developments, tougher regulations, or political agreements that we seek outside. The truly important and necessary changes are the ones *within* us.

Looking at the world through the eyes of coexistence, feeling the world with the heart of coexistence, and choosing actions based on the standard of coexistence—this is the beginning of real change. When we begin to make these changes within ourselves, many things in our lives change.

Just taking more interest in each other and being kinder to one another can make our lives safer and more peaceful. Simply eliminating material waste from our lives can bring us more relaxation and freedom and greatly reduce stress on the planet. Even without new technologies, institutions, or infrastructures, we can do a lot with these "soft" changes. We can change our lives and transform our communities and the global environment. What we need now is to make up our minds to create such changes in our own lives. This is the change we really need—and the way to save ourselves.

CHAPTER 2

A Connected World, a Divided Us

"If you want to go quickly, go alone.
If you want to go far, go together."

— African Proverb

Since the winter of 2019, the COVID-19 pandemic has been a trying, painful experience for all of us, no matter where in the world we live. The sacrifices we've had to make and the costs we've had to bear because of the pandemic have been tremendous. The pandemic continues despite all those sacrifices and expenditures, and experts predict that instead of disappearing, COVID is likely to remain a part of our lives, a continuing problem to which we must adapt and respond.

Time will soften the memory of what we experienced during the pandemic. Even the effects of intense experiences and recollections eventually fade, and associated emotions are diluted. The same will be true for the COVID pandemic, a crisis that has shaken us and uprooted our lives. Yet the realizations and wisdom we have gained through this ordeal will remain, causing us to grow.

What have we learned from the pandemic, individually and as a species? I hope the recent pandemic will leave us with more than just a sense of discomfort, more than a feeling of dread we want to shake off as quickly as possible. Instead, I hope it will be an opportunity to discover what values are truly precious to us, where our true strength lies, and how we can create a healthier, safer, and more sustainable world for everyone.

The Pandemic's Clear Reminder for Us

It's a familiar refrain: all of life is one connected whole. Almost all spiritual traditions have long stressed this message, repeatedly and emphatically. But, the interconnection of life isn't something you can only experience in quiet meditation. All of us have felt it to some degree at certain times. For instance, many will remember the shock of the financial crisis that started on Wall Street in New York in 2008 and spread through the whole world. Still, the claim that all life is an interconnected whole or that the world operates on a single system may feel abstract to some. If they've only experienced this indirectly, it may not seem real.

The COVID epidemic has been different, though. A new type of virus discovered in a Chinese city took no more than two or three months to develop into a pandemic, which shows how closely interconnected we are. Many of us have been infected, and we've seen others around us suffer from the infection. We've lost family, friends, and colleagues. As of October 2022, the number of people infected with COVID-19 worldwide exceeded 600 million, and deaths reached more than six million.

We saw it all happening on live TV, watching the numbers of infected growing, the infection spreading, its ravages reaching us from places around the globe. Everybody suffered a real lack of freedom; our residences, movement, and face-to-face interactions were limited to control the infection. Through the pandemic, all people experienced how interconnected the world is—feeling it viscerally, on a direct, personal level.

In almost all countries, wearing a mask has been one of the more uncomfortable things during the pandemic. Restrictions on travel and gatherings were a considerable inconvenience, but masks were particularly unpleasant; the masks "hit us where it hurts" in the most fundamental of biological activities—obstructing our breathing, suffocating us.

Controversy surrounded mask-wearing in many countries. In the United States, positions on the obligatory wearing of masks varied according to the political proclivities of each state. Many people's first reaction was to say, "I'm fine, so why do I have to wear an uncomfortable mask?" It took a while to sink in that wearing a mask isn't just about *you*; it's for the sake of others who might be infected through you. It took even longer for people to accept that doing this would ultimately protect them, too.

On the other hand, the discomfort of wearing a mask enabled us to feel the value of clean air and the importance of breathing. That discomfort—the inability to breathe as we want, the most fundamental freedom a living thing can have—is hard to express in words.

With money, we buy water and food. We each have a cup for drinking our water and a bowl for eating our food. But we don't each have a container for the air we breathe. Wherever we go, we all breathe air from one large container used by all humankind—the atmosphere. What could better show us that our lives all share a single root? The breaths we take each moment show us how deeply connected we are to one another. Probably the most valuable lessons we can learn from the pandemic are that we are all deeply connected and that, as a result, protecting others is protecting ourselves. We should remember this each and every time we take a breath.

This is not a lesson that applies only during a pandemic. Whether it's the worldwide logistics disruption caused by the collapse of the supply chain since the pandemic, interest-rate adjustments and the threat of inflation caused by government expansion of the money supply, or the global exchange-rate war, these situations all lead to the same conclusion: we are deeply connected to each other.

Therefore, the lesson that protecting others is protecting ourselves can be applied to everything forming the basis of our lives, including environmental pollution, climate change, social safety, and information management. Expanding this further, we come to a much deeper realization: working for the good of others benefits me. All these experiences teach us to seek a way to live together, a way to coexist.

Sustainability Is Based on Communities

Sustainability has become a familiar term to most people, used for everything from product selection by individual consumers to national governmental policies. But we must remember that sustainability can only be realized at the community level. The life of an individual is not inherently sustainable. In the natural world, some species live solitary lives, except at certain times such as during the breeding season. Tigers are an example of this. However, many more animal species live in groups and often form well-organized communities. The most prominent example is us, of course—humanity.

It is obvious that humans are superior to other species in intelligence as we define it and have gained an advantage over other creatures, for instance, by using fire and tools. However, such advantages aren't all that useful for individuals. Modern humans are a species capable of using knowledge and technologies incomparable to anything in the past, but even with all our accomplishments, an individual thrown out into nature on his or her own would be unlikely to survive. We are currently thriving in the global ecosystem not because individual humans are impressive but because we are strong as a species. We enjoy our present status on the world stage not as individuals but as members of a formidable group: humanity.

The history of evolution consistently shows how much more powerful sociality is than individual ability. Neanderthals—*Homo neanderthalensis*—are the closest known species to modern humans, *Homo sapiens*. How Neanderthals, who lived alongside our ancestors, vanished and left us as a single species remains a mystery. Recently discovered biological data suggest Neanderthals had larger and stronger skeletons than *Homo sapiens*. Considering brain capacity, which can be inferred from skull size, and the level of tools Neanderthals seem to have used, we cannot conclude that they were inferior to us in intelligence, either. While *Homo sapiens* originally came up from warm climates, Neanderthals survived in harsher, more barren surroundings and are presumed to have been more adaptable to the environment.

So why were Neanderthals, who seemed to be at an evolutionary advantage in every way, pushed aside by *Homo sapiens*? One widely accepted explanation is the difference in sociability. Being more sociable, *Homo sapiens* may have become more accustomed to cooperation and a division of labor, enabling them to form larger groups. No matter how outstanding Neanderthals were as individuals, the difference in group size would have left them unable to compete.

We can see a similar historical example in the competition between nomadic and agricultural peoples. Sweeping away all before them to conquer vast territories, nomadic people often outperformed agricultural people in personal fighting power. But in terms of sociality, division of labor, and cooperation, and in the size of the groups that can be created under such conditions, the nomads were inferior to the agriculturalists. As a result, agriculture-based communities now predominate.

The most significant reason humans can dominate other species is our ability to cooperate socially and communicate. So, it is ironic that the closest, most significant threat to humanity—one that could cause the collapse of human society—is conflict within the species. This is confirmed by the war in Ukraine, the talk of the competition for supremacy between the United States and China, and even the threatened use of nuclear weapons.

The biggest crises we face are climate change and environmental destruction. However, a more stable climate and a healthier environment will not necessarily lead to human sustainability. Conflicts within human societies threaten human sustainability as much as environmental factors, perhaps even more so. There is no sustainable future for us unless we find a way to resolve the conflicts within human society and learn to live together.

What Makes a Community Safe and Healthy?

Thanks to the development of high-speed communication technologies, it doesn't take much time to know what's happening anywhere on the planet. We can get information from distant countries with just a few clicks. We can buy products made in those places and have video chats in real time with people on the other side of the planet.

Since distance is no longer an obstacle to communication and exchange, most people find other countries and cultures much less strange than they once did. Even distant countries we've never visited now feel like nearby cities. We can vividly see the lives of the people there through YouTube, and it's easy to interact directly. As a result, the world feels much smaller.

What's easy to miss in these communication networks is the *quality* of the connections, not the quantity. According to Facebook data, as of 2021, 2.9 billion active users access their Facebook pages at least once a month. That's 36 percent of the world's eight billion people. The average number of "friends" per person is 340, and the total number of individual friends is more than 100 times the global population. In other words, the world's social network comprises many interconnected layers of friends. If 36 percent of the worldwide population is bound together by friendship, then the earth should be a utopia, with few enemies to be found anywhere. Unfortunately, crimes stemming from violence, terrorism, discrimination, and hatred never cease.

Recently, something has been getting attention as a new factor threatening health: loneliness. As a problem, loneliness is considered more severe than smoking, obesity, or lack of exercise. Studies have shown that a lack of close social connections can increase mortality by as much as 26 percent. This is equivalent to smoking 15 cigarettes per day. How paradoxical is it that so many are dying of loneliness in this world full of friends?

We eagerly share our daily lives with countless friends through various social media platforms, not only Facebook. But how many of them share our dreams and feel our pain? A real connection isn't the number of friends you have or the number of likes your post gets on social media. External links without any inner connection only make people feel lonelier.

To create authentic relationships, we need to learn to trust and care for one another and share a common dream for the earth and humanity. Even seemingly beneficial, high-profile connections are no more than trappings papered over the mess of our lives if they lack mutual trust, consideration, care, and shared goals and values.

Research into what factors significantly affect quality of life in a community has produced some fascinating results. What do you think most impacts overall quality of life in a community—safety, crime rates, job opportunities, public health? Security systems, the number of police officers, community members' educational levels, income, businesses providing numerous jobs? All of these are important, of course. But according to many studies, there are other factors with the same or greater influence.

These are "how many people know each other's names" and "how often they interact in public spaces." Stated more simply, it's how much people care about each other. It starts simply with knowing who each other is. An example is greeting someone by name when you meet on the street or in a marketplace. This seemingly straightforward element gives people a feeling of belonging to a community and motivates a sense of responsibility for one another. We want to help others around us who are in need and makes us less likely to harm other members of the community.

When I was young, rural villages were small, and we knew each other's family circumstances well. To exaggerate a little, neighborhood women even knew the number of chopsticks next door because they'd go to help when there were big events, such as weddings or funerals. When adults saw children being rude or misbehaving, either their own kids or those of others, they would scold them. "Do your parents know what you're doing?" they would ask, giving the youngsters an earful. This was an expression of concern and care, not criticism. In such an environment, misbehaving isn't easy unless you're a bit of a jerk!

Korea is not alone in this. In the United States, a saying from Africa has become popular: "It takes a village to raise a child." Similarly, we find the Korean expression: "A disease is healed only by spreading the word about it." For this proverb to make sense, you must live in a community whose members care about each other. Otherwise, the disease is a private matter that must be kept hidden; letting people know about it may result in discrimination.

Many individuals in communities today are less about caring for their neighbors and more about "keeping up with the Joneses." They commute long hours to jobs in the cities that help pay mortgages in fancy neighborhoods in the suburbs where no one talks to each other. Often, they don't even know each other's names! Lacking mindfulness and care for one another, this sort of community is like a body without a spirit.

The greatest power making a community safer, healthier, and more sustainable is the compassion flowing between us, from heart to heart. This applies across the board, from the smallest village to human society, and to all living things. Developing and expanding this mindset can make the world more harmonious and sustainable.

Physical conditions allowing people to connect through compassion, regardless of spatial distance, have already been created here on Earth. As the use of social media has increased and many people have shared their lives with others, we have gotten used to the fact that ways of living and thinking different from our own exist in the world. And we can now connect and interact with people we feel emotionally close to regardless of spatial distance. Through such interactions, tremendous changes are taking place in the ways we define community, where the geographical limitations of space were once an important factor.

In addition to traditional local communities, new communities of another dimension are emerging, free of geographical limitations. The networks and social media that connect the world today allow us to create holistic communities where information and emotion flow together. In our experience of the pandemic, we've clearly seen the possibilities. The key, however, is found in people's hearts, not in technology or infrastructure. In Korea, this spirit is known as Hongik—the intention to care for the world, not just for ourselves—and this spirit is what makes the earth a true community, a global village.

CHAPTER 3

The Inner Guide to Coexistence

*"In recognizing the humanity of our fellow beings,
we pay ourselves the highest tribute."*

— Thurgood Marshall

Do you think it would be possible to change the future of mankind just by changing our mindset? It might sound too simple, but the human mind is where all change begins and where all solutions come from.

When it comes to what the mind is—where it exists, and how—we do not yet have an explanation that everyone agrees upon. In psychology and neuroscience, for the most part, the mind is not considered an objectively existing entity but rather a phenomenon created by brain activity. On the other hand, some spiritual traditions teach that the mind is a fundamental real thing, and that everything in the world is a kind of illusion that happens within it. But one thing is clear: it is through the workings of the brain that we recognize and experience the mind. This makes the brain an important starting point for deeply studying and observing the mind.

I became interested in the brain early on. It wasn't out of curiosity about the amazing faculties of the brain. It was because those faculties didn't work as well for me as I wanted them to. As a youth, I had problems concentrating. I struggled so much that I had trouble reading books properly in class at school. Looking at a book for just a few minutes made the letters get up and move around as if they were alive, and the inside of my head became cluttered as I tumbled into an abyss of one thought leading to another and yet another. At the time, I thought I wasn't as diligent as my friends or had a weak will, and I blamed myself. It wasn't until I had a deeper understanding of the brain that I realized this was happening due to of the state of my brain at the time.

Because of those struggles in my youth, I invested a lot of attention and effort in self-reflection and self-control. In the process, I came across various methods of mind-body training and self-discipline, including meditation, martial arts, and qigong. One of my biggest discoveries was the latent potential and creativity of the brain—the realization that the human brain has much greater capacity than most of us realize.

I have become convinced that by awakening and utilizing the latent potential of the brain, we can both improve our quality of life as individuals and contribute to creating a more peaceful and sustainable future for humankind. I now view the development of the human brain as a basic life skill that everyone should understand and apply in order to live their best possible life. Thus, I have spent most of my life creating a system of mind-body development called Brain Education, organizing it into an academic discipline, and sharing it with everyone I can.

The "brain" in Brain Education is, of course, the anatomical organ inside our heads. However, what is specifically taught and developed in Brain Education is not the brain as an organ, but the operations taking place *inside* the brain, which comprise what we call *mind*. The mind works whether you believe it is the root of existence and an underlying entity or if you think it's a phenomenon that occurs at the peak of brain activity.

The mind itself, unlike the brain, can neither be seen nor touched. But through the brain, and through the body connected with the brain, we can reach, feel, and affect the mind. Practices such as meditation, qigong, dance, breathwork, martial arts, hiking, and golf can all be excellent tools for observing, feeling, and influencing the mind. I was once asked to give the simplest definition of Brain Education, and my reply was this: "It's how to use your mind."

The Most Powerful Medicine in the World

What do you think is the most powerful medicine in the world? If I pose this question at a workshop, people offer various responses, such as laughter, love, or food—all reasonable answers. There is, however, a medicine that is much more powerful than any of these: the power of the mind.

It usually takes more than 10 years for a pharmaceutical company to develop a new drug. This process usually goes through three stages of testing. The first stage typically involves testing for safety with a small group of subjects. The second and third stages test for efficacy, starting with comparisons between control groups and test groups. The new drug must pass all the tests before it can be approved by the FDA, be mass-produced, and be distributed to consumers. The probability of passing all the tests and being commercialized is less than 10 percent.

One of the most stringent tests in the second and third phases is comparison of the drug with a placebo, or "fake" pill. A pill that doesn't contain the medicinal ingredient is given to test subjects who believe it's the real medicine, and then the group that took the placebo is compared with a group that took the actual drug. But many test products fail when they don't prove to be any more effective than the placebo. Of course, some show greater effectiveness than the placebo, but far more of them fail the test.

If we average the test results of all drugs and statistically compare that to the efficacy of the placebo, it wouldn't be wrong to say that the placebo is the most powerful medicine in the world. It must be truly disappointing if a drug developed over a long time with massive investments fails because it doesn't show a better effect than a lump of sugar-coated flour. The placebos are effective because the subjects' minds *believe* that it is the real medicine and that it can cure their condition.

The power of the mind—which makes the placebo effect possible—is manifested in everything that involves our minds. It is working behind the information that we encounter every day, as well as in all our choices and actions.

For example, there have been experiments comparing academic achievement when teachers have positive expectations that their students will do well and when they expect the opposite. The results show that students on the receiving end of positive expectations demonstrate higher achievement.

Of course, there may be several factors at work here. First, there may be a difference in how teachers look at students—their facial expressions—and speak to them when they have positive as opposed to negative expectations. There could also be a difference in the degree of interest, care, and time invested by the teachers toward their students. This is essentially no different from our expectations of the placebo since the teacher's mind creates the effect, which in turn influences the students' minds about themselves and their ability to learn.

Despite great advances in neuroscience, we do not yet know the full extent of the power of the mind. There are so many variables in life that it is difficult to obtain the same kind of objective data as we have for the placebo effect. It is clear, however, that what's at work behind both the placebo effect and having positive expectations toward students is the power of the mind. This is the most powerful tool we can use to change our own lives and change the world.

The Three Treasures of the Mind

The human mind possesses an amazing power for creation. Placebos are a very limited example of that. Depending on how you use the power of your mind, you could either help yourself and others or you could be destructive to yourself and others. Fortunately, we have guides within us to help us use the power of our minds in a good way. These guides are empathy, conscience, and introspection—three traits of our minds that guide us to go beyond the limits of ego to take the path of coexistence.

Empathy: Feeling the Pain of Others

Empathy means feeling another person's emotions and understanding their thoughts and perspectives. When other people feel positive emotions, such as joy or pleasure, we can share those feelings. Even when they feel negative emotions, like sadness or pain, we can resonate with and feel those emotions, too.

What if you saw someone walking down the street and they suddenly slammed very hard into something, or you saw someone slip on ice and fall hard on the ground? Wouldn't your own body get tense and your face express pain, as if you were the one who'd run into something or fallen? In studies on this subject, scientists repeatedly reach the same conclusion. The area of the brain that is activated when you feel your own pain is the same area activated when you see others experience pain. Scientists say this is because of the mirror neurons in our brains, and they speculate that these may be the neurological basis for empathy.

It is not yet clear whether mirror neurons really are the basis for empathy, and we're not entirely sure whether empathy is a trait demonstrated only by humans. However, studies confirm that our brains are designed to empathize with the feelings we observe in other people as if they are our own. Empathy can be improved and developed through learning, but it's a characteristic inherent in our brains.

According to studies of nature, many animals and even plants, which lack brain-like neural networks, are known to exhibit behaviors similar to empathy. For example, in a pride of lions hunting as a group, it was observed that rather than attacking a baby impala that suddenly appeared in front of her, a lioness would protect it from another lion's attack. Monkeys were seen signaling deer by sound so they could avoid an approaching leopard. And it is becoming increasingly known that plants also exhibit electro-chemical signals in the presence of the suffering of other plants, which look like empathetic responses.

In a way, rather than being an ability per se, empathy seems closer to a sense of life shared by all living things. It is tremendously hopeful that all living things may have as a basic sense the ability to empathize with one another. This means that we have the potential to realize harmonious coexistence not only within human society but with all life systems existing on earth.

In terms of the breadth of empathy and the range of actions we can take, though, humans cannot be compared with other animals or plants. It's hard to expect animals to feel the conditions of animals and plants on another continent across the ocean. On the other hand, humans have the power to empathize not only with people close to them but all living beings.

It was actually because of this power of empathy that many beverage stores stopped using plastic straws. A few years ago, a marine life research team from Texas A&M University found a sea turtle off the coast of Costa Rica that was struggling to breathe. They saw something blocking the turtle's nostril, made a video of the process of taking it out, and posted it on YouTube. In the video, the turtle's nose bleeds, and he keeps making painful sounds. The team removes a plastic drinking straw that had ended up in the ocean and become stuck in this sea turtle's nostril. The video went viral, was viewed by more than 100 million people in a short time, and became the impetus for a worldwide campaign to ban the use of plastic straws in restaurants.

We have known for a long time that plastic is harmful to the environment and the waste we throw away affects the marine ecosystem. But, seeing the turtle suffering as he shed blood and people working so hard to pull out the straw stuck in his nose hit us at a different level.

Having an intellectual understanding of something doesn't immediately tie into action. But *feeling* it is different. It's not the thought that water is important and that you need it, but the dryness and thirst you feel in your throat that makes you jump up from your seat to get water. It isn't simply knowledge but rather feelings that drive people to choose and act. This is the difference between intellectual understanding and emotional empathy. The story of the sea turtle shows that the power of empathy is real.

Empathy makes seeing the pain of others feel like one's own pain, and it is because we have empathy that we naturally feel a desire to help when we see people in need. This is what makes us automatically reach out a hand when someone next to us falls. If a wounded animal is suffering, we go over to look. When a natural disaster happens and many are suffering and in pain, people hurry to volunteer their help, even if they have no personal connection to them. When other people, plants and animals, mountains and rivers, oceans and the sky feel like part of ourselves, we naturally come to have the mind that respects and cherishes them and take action to protect and heal them.

When empathy becomes deeper, it is expressed as compassion. The word for *compassion* in Korean is *jabi*, with *ja* meaning "love" and *bi* meaning "sadness." Thus, compassion is loving sadness. In English, the word *passion* refers to "suffering," and the prefix *com* means "with," so having compassion means that one is suffering along with the other. So, both languages suggest that feeling compassion is to feel the pain that another is feeling, which leads naturally to a thoughtful and loving mind that wants to ease that pain.

When we are happy, it doesn't bother us too much if no one recognizes our happiness. But with sadness and pain, it's different. Often, when I'm struggling and in pain, it's comforting just to have someone there by my side or simply listening quietly to what I'm saying. The times when we really need empathy are when we feel sad and hopeless, or we're in pain, having a hard time.

How do you feel when other people understand what you are feeling? Feeling that someone else has listened to you and understands how you feel leaves a deep impression, even if it has only happened once. For me, experiences like this make life more bearable and worth living, even if that other person hasn't done anything specific to change my situation. This is the power of empathy, the power of compassion. It connects our minds, lends us comfort and strength, and heals wounds.

Conscience: Our Will to Truth

Along with the compassion that comes from empathy, there is within us a characteristic that we refer to as "conscience." Why do some people retain their integrity and goodness even in situations where it may cause personal disadvantage or loss? Why do we feel uncomfortable when we don't listen to the voice of our conscience?

What is most surprising about conscience is that *everyone* has one, regardless of bloodline, education, or living conditions. This shows that conscience, like our instincts, is an essential part of human nature. Conscience, however, is different from morality, ethics, and social norms, which vary depending on social, cultural, and historical context.

Conscience is not something we gain through effort or self-discipline. It's something that is simply given to us. Conscience is a mirror that reflects truthfulness, and it motivates us to direct ourselves toward truthfulness. It gives us the will to do what is right, no matter the circumstances. It is the inner purity, the bright light within that was originally given to each of us. We may be able to ignore the voice of conscience, but we cannot deny the *existence* of conscience, because conscience is rooted in everyone's nature.

The voice of conscience is simple and straightforward. That's why following your conscience doesn't require much logic or explanation. On the other hand, complex logic or lengthy explanations are necessary to justify and rationalize choices that do *not* follow conscience.

Because of conscience, each of us has the potential for greatness. It's because of the undeniable presence of conscience that we can choose the side of truthfulness, even if that choice may result in personal disadvantage. We can choose the action that is altruistic, brave, bold, creative, and great, though to the eyes of ego it might seem irrational to do so. It's not because the ego isn't smart but because it thinks only of itself that it is unable to make the best choice.

Everyone has a conscience, so having one doesn't mean we have achieved greatness. That is determined by whether we make the choice to acknowledge the existence of conscience and follow its guidance. Conscience as an expression of absolute truthfulness is found within everyone. Acknowledging its voice is the beginning of wisdom; living it is virtue.

The Power of Introspection: The Mind That Asks, "Who Am I?"

The mind's power of introspection, which we normally call "mindfulness," enables us to detect signals of conscience and compassion and to listen to that voice. This is one of the mind's instinctive capacities, one that is demonstrated well when, in a state of relaxed concentration, the mind is unhindered by thoughts or emotions.

What thoughts or feelings are passing through your mind right now? If you have a paper and pen nearby, try writing them down. What did you notice when you were asked this question and observed your inner world? Did you have the odd experience of feeling that while ordinarily your head is full of thoughts, whether you want them or not, once you try to observe them, there's nothing to write down?

The consciousness that observes has the power to silence thought. If you hadn't tried to force yourself to think about something, you would suddenly have encountered an empty space of consciousness when looking at what your thoughts or feelings are right now. But you may not have noticed this emptiness because you were looking for thoughts.

We experience the existence of the mind through our thoughts and emotions. When a clear glass wall is being installed at a construction site, a sign reading "Watch out for glass" might be posted lest people bump into it without realizing it is there. If the glass is very clear and standing by itself, its existence isn't perceived, so we are made aware of it by the warning. Our mind is just like that glass. However, since we almost always perceive and experience the mind through our thoughts and emotions, we mistake them for our mind.

Faced with observation by a consciousness that's awake, thoughts and emotions vanish like fog in the morning sun. What remains is not tangible, and it has no shape or form. It has no smell and no boundary, so it cannot be said to be large or small, and its beginning and end cannot be known. It may even be impossible to say whether it is absent or present. That is your mind, your pure consciousness.

A mind that is transparent and open in this way makes it possible for us to see the true nature of things, undistorted by our preconceptions, desires, or emotions. We are conscious of our own existence and have questions concerning our existence because of the mind's capacity for introspection. This is what makes us ask questions such as "Who am I?" and "Where did I come from?" and constantly seek answers through the lives we live.

As has been the case for many spiritual teachers through-out human history, the power of introspection may lead to great enlightenment. Even if it doesn't, we attain big and small insights in our daily lives through introspection. We observe our inner thoughts and external actions and get feedback from the self-awareness attained through that observation.

Our Tools for a Life of Coexistence

Among all the organs in our bodies, the brain is the one that changes the most. New connections are made between the nerves every moment through our thoughts, emotions, sensations, and experiences. Existing connections are strengthened or may become weak and disappear. Presumably the powers of empathy, conscience, and introspection in our brains are no different. As with other brain capabilities, these increase with use but weaken and degenerate without use.

Empathy guides us to live in harmony with all other people and life forms. But to develop this precious ability, we need to actively use it. If the circuits for empathy in the brain have grown weak from lack of use, like weakened muscles, we need to revive them.

Empathy, conscience, and the power of introspection are like a compass for leading a life of coexistence. The beautiful and noble mind that looks inside and outside oneself with a consciousness that's always awake, that goes beyond gains and losses and strives to be true, and that seeks to lessen the suffering of other people and other life forms—this mind leads us to make the right choices no matter what the situation. When these three elements are combined, we can make choices that benefit everyone. Such choices lead to coexistence, which saves us all. These three powers of the mind provide the basis for the hope that we can embrace for a better future.

Meditation, the Path to Finding the Mind

By following the guidance of the three treasures of the mind, we can make good choices that benefit everyone and move toward realizing coexistence. These inner guides also lead us to the mind itself, the root and true foundation of these guides. You can focus on empathy and practice compassion, follow conscience in pursuit of the truth, or seek enlightenment through introspection. But all three ultimately have the same destination: the mind itself. Depending on which of these you focus, there are various practices—such as prayer, meditation, service, and study—that can be used and have been used in different spiritual traditions.

Meditation is at once the simplest and most direct and universal way for us to listen to the voices of our inner guides and find our minds. To meditate doesn't mean adding anything but rather setting down all the things you were doing intentionally and returning to your original, natural state of being.

Even when you're not doing anything intentional, your heart beats and your breathing continues. Since your sensory organs are working, you can see the leaves swaying in the breeze and feel the wind brushing against your skin. You can sense the fragrance of flowers carried by the breeze. A thought might come to mind, or you might feel an emotion. All these things can happen without your doing them on purpose.

To meditate is to wake up and simply watch these things that happen in your mind without letting your mind stick to or follow anything. If you don't try to change or eliminate thoughts or emotions in your mind but simply watch them as they are—without weighing them as something you like or dislike—those thoughts and emotions will gradually subside.

As your thoughts and emotions abate, the gaps between them keep growing and the consciousness that is the background of the thoughts, rather than the thoughts themselves, will be increasingly perceived. This is the practice of the mind looking into the mind. As thoughts gradually subside and consciousness becomes more and more recognized, at a certain moment the distinction between consciousness as an object of recognition and consciousness as the agent of recognition disappears, leaving only the one consciousness. The self that observes and the self that is the object of observation merge into one. That is when all the distinctions between oneself and others, inside and outside, and humans and nature disappear, and we realize that such distinctions never existed in the first place.

Like space, the consciousness experienced at this time is essentially oneness that can't be divided. The boundary between the subjective self and the underlying reality has disappeared. This has been called "the consciousness of the zero point" and "the observer consciousness." Being an observer means becoming one with this foundational consciousness. In front of this bright and pure power of observation, all the illusions of falsehood and separation disappear, and true reality is revealed.

Although it is a very personal activity for each of us to observe our own mind through meditation, at the same time it means finding the common roots that connect all of us as one. Paradoxically, the deeper we go into our own individual selves, the more clearly we see that we are all connected. By confirming the single source that connects all of us deep in our minds, deep inside the consciousness we have seen through our brains, we find the power to heal division and make coexistence a reality.

The Noble Desire Within

There are inner guides within us, but we don't always follow them. What we listen to more often and more closely are the voices of our desires. We don't have to look that deeply inside ourselves for these desires to show up, demanding that they be seen and heard. And although the voices are diverse, the desires are derived from one common source— everyone's individual body and the idea rooted in the body that the self exists as a separate being, which is essentially the ego. Some desires are so powerful that they can cause us to close our eyes and cover our ears, and even choose to harm others and destroy ourselves.

On the other hand, there is one very special and noble desire that stands out from these. This desire makes us have bigger dreams and push past our limits. This desire is the seed that drives us toward greatness.

There is a simple experiment that confirms this desire. Take a pen and paper, and ask yourself the following question: "How do I want to be remembered by other people when I leave this life?" Close your eyes for a moment, steady your breathing, pose this question to your mind, and quietly feel your heart. An answer will come from within. Write that down. I recommend that you not use the first person but instead refer to yourself in the third person, as "he" or "she."

This question has been used frequently in various forms in different self-development programs and social psychological studies. One interesting fact is that most people want to be remembered as "someone who helped the world," regardless of what kind of life they are living now and what kind of life they've lived in the past.

There is something very special about this question. If you ask, "What do I want most?" without any other conditions, you can't avoid having your attention be focused on that "I." But the condition of "when I leave this life" leads our consciousness to a desire from a place that's deeper than our personal wants or goals, and to a truth that is beyond the needs of this one mortal life. There, even if we didn't usually notice it all that well, we meet a noble desire that has always existed in us—a pure and good intention to help others and the world.

Feeling great joy and satisfaction in helping other people seems to be wired into the circuits of our brains. According to observations of the brain using magnetic resonance imaging (MRI), we feel happy when we help others. The act of helping others activates the same parts of the brain that are stimulated when we eat delicious food or have sex—in essence, the pleasure receptors.

The brain activation caused by helping others is sustained for much longer than that caused by food or sex. Deriving pleasure from delicious food or from sex requires direct stimulation. When that simulation is gone, we are left with feelings of loss and need. But memories of helping others and remembering that our presence was meaningful to someone bring the same sense of joy and happiness that we felt when we took that action.

The desire to help others and do things that are beneficial to the world is as basic as the desire for food or sex. This desire, like the desire for food or for sex, exists beyond individual personality or ego or character. Having such mechanisms in our brains shows us the way we can reach continuous growth and long-lasting happiness.

When we have a desire to help someone—to do something beneficial for the world—this noble desire stirring within us may feel unfamiliar. You might even say to yourself, "Now, why would I do that?" as you turn away from the thought of it. However, remember that the desire to serve the greater good exists within you, independent of your personality, your present life condition, or your current lifestyle, just as your desire for food or sex does. Recognizing that this drive is as important as the drive for food and sex is the beginning of change. Fortunately, no talent, skill, or accomplishment is needed. Simply accepting and choosing this noble consciousness awakens the latent potential of the brain that leads to a life of harmonious coexistence.

Even now, there are many people on Earth who believe that one day someone will suddenly appear to save the world and be their salvation. Meanwhile, the world situation grows increasingly difficult by the minute. The origins of many religions began with the advent of such saviors, prophets, and messiahs. But, I don't think we can afford to wait for just one special or supernatural being.

We all need to step up. Our earth is asking for not just one individual or a couple of people, but for many people who declare, "I will save the earth and save the world." Fortunately, more people are embracing this mentality and choosing such actions. The way I see it, the more people we have like that, the better. I hope desperately for 100 million such people.

From deep in your heart, feel the noble desire to be someone who helps the world. Follow where your inner guides lead you, and find, choose, and carry out ways to realize that desire. That's what makes life meaningful and valuable, and it makes this earth a healthier, more beautiful, and better place on which to live.

PART 2

Earth-Centered Consciousness

CHAPTER 4

The Mind that Feels the Earth

"There is no Wi-Fi in the forest, but I promise you will find a better connection."

— Anonymous

If I were to ask you to feel your heart right now, what kind of gesture would you make? Most people would place their hands on their chests. We usually take in information this way—through our five senses. Light, touch, tastes, smells, and sounds stimulate our senses, and our brain interprets this stimulation, resulting in thoughts, emotions, and physiological reactions such as our gut clenching or our breathing speeding up.

All of these stimulations, thoughts, and feelings, however, are just the tip of the iceberg of what we can sense. Often, we are so bombarded by them, though, that we have no idea there is more to discern beneath the torrent of perceptions and reactions.

All of us have an inner wisdom that cannot be accessed with our five senses or understood by intellectual analysis. It can only be "felt" by an inner sense that we may already be aware of but have not fully accessed. We can use this sense to feel the reactions of our conscience and of our body, which let us know what's good for us. Since we are connected at the most fundamental level with other life forms and the earth itself, this inner feeling can also point us toward what would be good for everyone.

Integrating the subtle guidance of feeling into our lives makes our experiences deeper and more aligned with who we are. It's difficult to say we've really experienced something without feeling anything, whether it's a daily activity or relationships with people. Feeling also gives us motivation to act. After all, it isn't knowing how good water is for your body but rather the feeling of thirst that usually makes you drink it.

We may not normally think of getting a feeling for the earth, and it may be hard to feel because it's too close or too big. For most of us, the earth is more like an abstract concept than a concrete object or an inner sense. That's why we meet the earth through data, policies, slogans, and agendas instead of recognizing its existence through experiencing it.

The Earth as an Agenda

A historic global Climate Change Conference hosted by the United Nations was held in Paris in December 2015. At this conference, 195 countries adopted an agreement that was to take effect starting in 2020. Each participating country set a goal and submitted a pledge to achieve that goal. Previously, the UN's goal had been to ensure that global atmospheric temperatures would not rise more than 2.0°C, as proposed in Copenhagen in 2009. But, because many experts determined that this was not enough, at the Paris conference, the goal was strengthened to limit global warming temperatures to well below that, as close as possible to 1.5°C.

However, the agreement from the Paris Climate Change Conference—considered the last hope to prevent a catastrophic end—nearly became a meaningless piece of paper due to lack of cooperation on the part of the nation-states in power. It is surprising that an agreement made with such difficulty could be so easily destroyed by changes in political leadership and interests. What's even more surprising is that many people don't take the global warming situation seriously.

Because the changes that take place in the vast systems of the earth are so big and so slow, it can be hard for us to sense these changes with our bodies. Because of the size and inertia of this massive system, once change has started, it is difficult or nearly impossible to shift its direction before it reaches a new equilibrium on its own.

We don't know exactly how long it takes for ocean currents or the atmospheric circulation to change direction. The point at which damage is irreversible could be 20 to 30 years from the onset of the change, or it could be sooner. It may have passed already. But hegemonic competition and trade conflicts are making international cooperation fall apart. Even Europe, which has been most proactive in dealing with the climate change crisis, is increasing its coal consumption due to the pandemic and the energy crisis caused by the war in Ukraine.

Despite the large amount of data warning of crisis, the awareness with which we see the problems and our responses to them are shockingly clumsy. We may think we still have time because we don't yet feel a sense of crisis in our bodies. Maybe people feel that the problem is just too big for any one individual to worry about. Or maybe the problem is so overwhelmingly big that people are waiting in a haze of uncertainty for someone to come and solve it for them.

But it is an irresponsible thought to expect that someone will magically come and solve these sustainability problems for us without our putting in individual efforts to reflect on and change our own consciousness, value systems, and lifestyles. Underpinning this idea is the thought that we are separate from nature. There is also the preconception that there isn't much an individual can do about the massive changes in the global environment, and that the major systems that drive the world are unaffected by the choices I make.

I Am Nature

What image comes to mind when you close your eyes and imagine nature? Many people think of green mountains, valleys with clear water, or beaches with fine sand. Some might imagine lightning ripping through the sky or mountainous waves swelling below crashing thunderstorms. While these certainly are aspects of nature that we can see, they represent a limited view of nature.

Many people forget that we ourselves are part of nature. Nature is not only the green forests that we drive out to see on weekends or the storms that we experience a few times a year. Nature is not something separate from us. Our breath, the living microbes in our intestines, the warm blood flowing through our blood vessels with the pulse of our heartbeat—these are all nature. *My life itself* and your life are part of nature.

Nature within you works with its own rhythm with no conscious effort from you. With the help of nature inside you, you maintain your body temperature, heal injuries over time, and recover when you catch the flu. But, as we have grown so accustomed to artificial things, we have forgotten the fact that we are nature, and thus we have become cut off from the rhythm of nature within us. This results in higher levels of stress, weakened natural healing, and an increasing dependence on external information and systems.

Sustainable living is not beyond our reach, but it starts with restoring our awareness of nature within ourselves. When our connection to nature inside of us recovers, our sense of the harmony and balance that life possesses comes alive again. When that sense of harmony and balance is revived, we can take better care of the health of our bodies and our minds. Being in that state revives our ability to empathize with others and feel their pain as our own pain. The objects of such empathy could be close family members or colleagues, animals and plants, or the earth itself. But when we're disconnected from the rhythm of life and have accumulated stress, we don't have the mental space to feel or comprehend the suffering of others. Even if we did, it would be hard to provide real help.

Statistics on climate change drive home the seriousness of the problem. Undoubtedly, we must enact new regulations to reduce carbon emissions. But we must also restore our sense of nature within us. When our inner sense of nature is restored, it leads us to make choices that are beneficial to ourselves, beneficial to others, and beneficial to the earth's environment. Feeling nature within ourselves recovers our sense of coexistence, and recovering that sense leads us to live sustainable lives and create a sustainable world.

The Earth and Me

The "overview effect" is one example of individuals experiencing dramatic changes in their feelings about their relationship with the earth. An example of this perspective shift occurs when astronauts view the earth from a distance and feel its beauty, preciousness, and fragility. Many people, including Yuri Gagarin, the Soviet cosmonaut who was the first human to travel in space, said they felt a deep sense of connection to the earth after traveling in space, and their values changed significantly as a result.

More recently, William Shatner, an American actor who turned 90 in 2021, reminisced about his own trip into space. He is widely known for his role as the captain of the starship *USS Enterprise* in the popular 1960s American drama *Star Trek*. In 2021, he went on a suborbital space flight at the invitation of Amazon founder Jeff Bezos, who had been a big fan of *Star Trek* as a child. Shatner and his fellow astronauts flew up 65.8 miles to the boundary of space, just past the edge of Earth's atmosphere, and experienced zero gravity for three to four minutes while seeing the earth from space. It was a short 10 minutes from takeoff to landing. In the memoir he published a year later, *Boldly*

Go, this is how Shatner described what he felt during that short journey into space:

> *When I looked in the opposite direction, into space, there was no mystery, no majestic awe to behold . . . all I saw was death. I saw a cold, dark, black emptiness. It was unlike any blackness you can see or feel on Earth. It was deep, enveloping, all-encompassing. I turned back toward the light of home. I could see the curvature of Earth, the beige of the desert, the white of the clouds and the blue of the sky. It was life. Nurturing, sustaining, life. Mother Earth. Gaia.*

He confessed that he felt overwhelming sadness watching the stark contrast between the cold darkness of space and the earth, emanating warmth. He said he felt alarmed by the increasing destruction of the earth and countless life forms becoming extinct at our hands every day.

What Shatner saw may not have been the truest representation of space, and in the distant future we might even discover space to be more beautiful and receptive than he described. But before such a discovery is made, we must take our first steps with hesitation and fear—like a baby taking its first steps or a child venturing beyond its neighborhood for the first time—as if we are trailblazers at the edge of a great canyon, cutting our way across to the place of a new settlement. And that's when we become aware of the vast sphere of protection and love in which we've been living, and how inextricably linked we are to that love and protection.

What's at the core of this change of heart, demonstrated in the overview effect, is having awareness of the earth as a single, whole unit and feeling the connection of life that links the earth and our individual selves. Fortunately, looking at Earth from space is not the only way this change can happen. The change actually happens in the mind, not in outer space. When such change takes place in our minds, not only does it change the way we look at the earth, but our attitude toward all people and all life forms change.

Earth Sensibility

Feeling that you're connected to the earth requires intellectual understanding, but more fundamentally, your ability to sense it must awaken. It requires effort to expand empathy beyond the people around you to the natural environment. We could call this ability "environmental sensibility" or "earth sensibility." It's more than understanding that we need our natural environment to be healthy; it's recognizing ourselves as part of that natural environment. It's feeling that the condition of the natural environment is the condition of our own bodies. This emotional and sensory connection with the earth helps transform knowledge about the environment into action on behalf of the earth.

About 10 years ago, I recommended doing handstand walking as an effective way to be healthy. I advised men to build up to walking 100 steps on their hands and women 50 steps on their hands. I practiced handstand walking myself and found it to be an effective exercise that not only builds muscle strength but also awakens people's sense of balance and corrects their alignment.

While recommending handstands, I added a special instruction—to do handstands with the intention of "holding up the earth." The idea of what is up or down is a gravitational illusion of sorts, based on the human point of view. From the perspective of the earth itself, or from the perspective of space, there is no "above" or "below." When I'm standing on my hands, I'm literally standing in space and holding up the earth. My idea behind "holding up the earth" was to help people feel a sense of responsibility for the earth, the same as they would feel the weight of their body while doing a handstand.

How can you feel the earth? Actually, there is never a moment when you're *not* feeling the earth. You don't have to hug a large tree deep in a forest or walk barefoot in the dirt. Whether you're sitting, lying down, walking, or even flying in an airplane, you're feeling the earth. The solid foundation supporting your buttocks and feet is the earth. The resistance that you feel when you swirl your hands in the air is the earth. The water cupped in your hands when you wash your face is the earth.

But we don't recognize those sensations as the earth because the earth as a whole is too big for us to perceive with our senses. It's like the analogy of the "blind men touching an elephant." If you touch a part of an elephant without seeing its entire shape, you might describe the elephant as being shaped like a large column, a thick snake, or a long horn. If you cannot see the entirety of an object because it's too big, it's actually no different than touching it with your eyes closed. Of course, we can see the whole earth in pictures taken from space. But what we experience in response to this visual information is more intellectual understanding than feeling.

Feeling the earth, therefore, is not what we feel when we see the earth with our eyes or touch it with our hands. Rather, it's what we feel with our minds. Feeling with the mind doesn't mean waking up our spiritual senses with high-level training to see with our third eyes. Instead, love is what we need.

If you ordinarily practice meditation, bring the earth to mind, and meditate with the earth in your embrace. If you practice a religious faith, try praying for the earth and not just for yourself, your family, or your religious organization, even if only once a week. If you practice qigong or energy healing, try sending the healing energy of love to the earth, even if it's just once a week. If you take a walk every day, walk with the intention of massaging the earth with your feet, even if it's just once a week. If you are trying to lose weight, practice fasting for the planet, even if it's for just one meal a week, and donate the amount you saved by fasting to saving the earth's environment. Demonstrating care and love in this way is the beginning of feeling the earth with your heart.

When we care for and love anything, many changes take place in our behavior. If you love someone, you think of that person when you choose your actions, when you buy something, or eat something delicious, or even when you see something beautiful. You want that person to be healthy and happy, and if you experience something good, you want to share it. Amid the many choices and actions in your daily life, ask yourself, "Will my choice or action help the earth or harm it?" If you do so sincerely, you are feeling the earth. I am not looking to share specific information or knowledge through this book, but this very mindset.

The Earth Is Sick

If you ask children to imagine the earth and to feel it, you might see them cry. Ask them why, and they might say, "The earth is hurting" or "I feel sorry for the earth." An acquaintance of mine awoke early one morning to the sound of her seven-year-old daughter sniffling as she shed tears. Startled, she asked, "What's wrong? Are you sick?" and her daughter said, "Mom, the earth is hurting so much." Over and over again, I have seen children from different cultures and backgrounds show similar reactions.

The earth is sick right now. The earth is experiencing pain and suffering. This is the actual condition of the earth at this moment. We're the ones who have caused this pain, and we're the ones who can heal it. Our minds can embrace the earth and feel it. If we act now to heal the earth, it will be a blessing for everyone. If we fail to do so and the earth tries to recover balance on its own, it will be a disaster for humans beyond what we have ever experienced before.

To help the earth recover, we need the same sensibility we have when our parents or children are sick and in pain. This sensibility does not solely arise from our peripheral senses like sight, touch, or taste. Nor is it just cognitive intelligence that understands exactly what the earth's current problems are and how serious they are. This ability to sense includes everything you see with your eyes, think with your head, and feel with your heart. We *have* this capability. It is through care and love that this ability starts to be demonstrated. With care and love for the earth, let's *feel* the earth. Let's follow where those feelings guide us and do something, starting with the smallest actions.

CHAPTER 5

Accepting Contradictions and Differences

*"My humanity is bound up in yours,
for we can only be human together."*

— Desmond Tutu

You may have heard the story of the mother who had two sons, one making a living by selling straw sandals and the other by selling wooden clogs. With the livelihoods of her sons depending on opposite weather patterns, the mother never saw a worry-free day, fretting for the sandal-monger on rainy days and for the clog-monger on sunny days.

Even just two people can put you in a quandary. What if you had to worry about 10 people, or 100? What about thousands, or tens of thousands? And if the object of your concern is the whole world, how can you achieve harmony and balance, coordinating the different concerns, goals, and interests of each individual and group?

Not yet free of the shock of the COVID pandemic, the world is stumbling, rocked by the shock of war. While the combat is taking place in Ukraine, virtually the whole world is involved, directly or indirectly. Economic sanctions and disruptions in logistics systems and supply chains have affected almost everyone.

This situation makes two things clear to us. First, as was confirmed during the pandemic, we are inextricably linked to one another. Second, despite that, the paradigms of separation, competition, and domination still rule human society. Underlying this is the thought, "I am separate from the world." This notion is the perception of what we commonly call "the ego." This understanding exists in everyone's consciousness, but its roots are deep and old, beyond the measure of individual lives. We could say that this has been the source of all our troubles throughout human history, the root of all our diseases. All criminal activities that involve breaking rules and pursuing self-interest while harming others begin here. Stress, too, said to be the cause of all diseases, starts with reacting to external change as a threat to "me."

One of the most obvious measures of an individual's social maturity is the ability to resolve conflicts. Can we mediate and resolve disputes through dialogue and compromise in a way that protects each other's interests? Or do we attempt to solve things with shouting and punching? This is one criteria for distinguishing between maturity and immaturity, or between adults and children. The roles and responsibilities given to any individual depend on that person's capacity for conflict resolution. When people or groups can resolve conflicts only by violence, giving them great power poses a significant threat to everyone. This goes for large groups and nations as well as individuals.

Dealing with individual and collective egos is no longer only the business of those experiencing conflict. As egos collectivize and the interests of large groups collide, such clashes increasingly involve the question of survival for the entire human race. We are experiencing this vividly through Russia's invasion of Ukraine, the competition for hegemony and the arms race among the great powers, and the existing nuclear threat. No longer merely a nice dream, resolving our conflicts and living together in harmony has become a necessary condition for our survival, as is a sustainable global environment.

Separation Is an Illusion

As emphasized in Chapter 2, the various crises we are currently experiencing clearly show that we are connected to each other and inevitably influence one another, no matter where we live. It's not only at the level of experience and perception. These connections are much deeper and more far-reaching.

Not a single thing in this world exists by itself. I'm sitting in a chair right now, the chair is standing on the floor, and the floor is resting on the ground. Earth is moving in a stable orbit through the gravitational field created by the solar system's sun, moon, and other planets. These intertwined relationships continue indefinitely.

In our bodies, we find the same principle at work. The body is made up of organs and tissues, tissues are made of cells, and cells of smaller intracellular organelles. Cells break down further into molecules, atoms, and finally electrons and elementary particles; nothing exists in isolation. If a specific cell cuts off communication with other cells around it, trying to grow and reproduce inde-pendently, we call it cancer.

Expanding this connection outward, we encounter what appears to be an immense void. The stars and galaxies are points of light in the dark night sky. They are scattered so far apart, we would have to travel 25,000 years at the speed of light to make it to the next closest galaxy to ours.

Taking the connection inward, we discover the same thing. If you are in search of the basic unit of matter, seemingly solid lumps disappear, and everything becomes a wave of vibrating energy. Waves are the fundamental state of all matter. More precisely, matter exists as a field of energy with waves extending infinitely in all directions. Even if we were to divide matter into small pieces, what we encounter in the end is a vast void.

Space has no boundaries. Whether we divide objects into smaller and smaller pieces or expand our search outward, we encounter the same void. From the smallest thing in the world to the largest, wherever we look we discover no basis for the separate existence of anything, much less a "me."

All things appear and disappear, like fireflies, within a void full of waving energy. This is the cosmos that modern science has shown us. It is the same picture of the world seen through enlightenment in humanity's spiritual tradi-tions. That there is no separate, independently existing self is a scientific fact before it is a spiritual realization. Beliefs or thinking that deny this are as unscientific as the claims that the earth is the center of the universe and that the sun orbits the earth.

The Thought of "Me"

Everything is interconnected through the void, with nothing existing in isolation. So why do we perceive the self as a solid, separate entity?

In most cases, when the senses are stimulated and the mind is drawn to the object stimulating it, the sleeping "self" rises to the surface of consciousness, drawn by judgmental reactions, by likes and dislikes. In spiritual traditions, the stimulus of the senses by an object is often referred to as "contact," and the resulting attraction of the mind to the object is expressed as "attachment," which involves me and an object as separate entities.

Because contact creates attachment instantly, most of us fail to recognize that moment and consider our "self" to have always been there, when it actually appeared at the moment of attachment. Once the "self" rises to the surface of consciousness, "I" think and act as if I am controlling everything and always have. In that instant, our consciousness is trapped in a mold of separation, competition, and domination, which shapes our perceptions of everything.

Most of the moments we remember are times when we did something as ourselves. Everything I do—buying something, meeting someone, calling or sending a text— falls into this category, so it seems like I've lived as "me" all day. But in fact, we spend more time living without even thinking of "me." Most of the activities that happen inside us take place without any thought of "me."

My body breathes on its own without thinking of "me." The same goes for eating or walking or sleeping. For instance, when I sleep, I do not think of "me" except for the short time when I'm dreaming. Many functions we perform in our lives proceed without "me"—and they run more smoothly when "I" am not there. There is no "I" when great plays are made in team sports, for example. The athletes race toward a common goal, their bodies and minds moving as one. The same is true when we are united, working toward a common goal—and that's when our brains are in top form. The limitations that keep the brain from unleashing its potential vanish when there is no "I."

Recognizing that separation is an illusion and accepting that we are all one does not mean we have to become martyrs, giving our lives to save the world. The concept of a functionally separate self is actually very useful. Because of this awareness, I don't put food in someone else's mouth when I'm hungry or scratch the leg of the person beside me when mine itches. What's important is understanding that the separately existing self is not a fundamental reality, but rather a thought, an idea, a habit or a social convention. It's learned at some point in life through the personal development process and becomes tinted with customs and culture. It's a tacitly accepted, convenient function for getting on in the world. Remembering the limitation of self as a functional apparatus when we make important choices and judgments will help us make wise decisions beneficial to ourselves and to the world.

Accepting the Coexistence of Contradictions

Underlying the perspective that sees life as a competition and the world as relationships of conflict and confrontation, along with the illusion of separation, is a limited awareness incapable of accepting the coexistence of contradictions. This forms the basis of the destructive, unlimited competition and zero-sum games that dominate most economic activities, from personal investments to international trade.

Is the coexistence of contradictions simply a conceptual or supernatural notion? Or is it a vision of a transcendent world seen only in the meditations of high priests, men living far removed from reality, or preaching that "Form is emptiness; emptiness is form"?

In the fall of 2019, for the first time in computer history, Google experimentally demonstrated that quantum computers outperform traditional computers. In just 200 seconds, a quantum computer using just 52 qubits (quantum bits) solved a calculation that would have taken a traditional supercomputer 10,000 years. This was possible because of the difference in the fundamental nature of qubits and bits.

Bits used in traditional computers can be in one of two states, 0 or 1. Conversely, using quantum mechanical superposition (particles and waves existing in many places simultaneously), the qubits in a quantum computer can be in multiple states at the same time—a state of 0 and 1 as well as 0 *or* 1. This seemingly simple distinction creates a massive difference between traditional and quantum computers.

The difference between 0 and 1 in a quantum computer is not a matter of arithmetic, not $1 - 0 = 1$. Here the difference between 0 and 1 is the difference between existence and nonexistence. It is the most fundamental contradiction.

More importantly, this is not a special state existing only in quantum computer systems but a universal characteristic of all things. All objects can be both particles and waves at the same time. In other words, *the entire universe exists based on the coexistence of contradictions.* An important insight we can gain from the success of quantum computers is that accommodating the coexistence of contradictions makes an incredible difference in our ability to understand things and solve problems.

The condition of all life is itself a contradiction. To live is to die, and to die is to live. To have lived a day today is to have died a day today. But we all live embracing this contradiction.

Viewing a contradiction as irreconcilable is a limitation not of the contradiction itself but of our perception. Knowing that and finding a way to coexist is wisdom. One and zero are the two poles of existence. Could there be a greater contradiction in the universe than these two opposites? If being and nothingness, existence and nonexistence coexist—and that is exactly how the universe exists—could there be any contradiction in this world that is impossible for us to reconcile?

What's Good for All Is Good for Me

I've searched many spiritual teachings handed down through human history to find the wisdom to overcome confrontation and separation and to realize coexistence. While resonating with and feeling grateful for the wisdom of all these great teachings, I also feel responsible for sharing the Hongik spirit of Korea, which translates into "widely benefit all," especially because I see the practical implications of this teaching in dealing with our current challenges.

Compassion, benevolence, and love are all precious teachings, all wonderful virtues as a mindset and attitude toward others, handed down by humankind's great teachers. These are personal virtues that we must realize and develop through training and practice. Hongik also requires these personal virtues but goes much further. It emphasizes social action and its results. Hongik teaches us to change the world by helping and influencing others for good through practical application.

This teaching contains a magnanimity, confidence, and lofty spirit toward the greater world, as well as love for fellow humans and society. It tells us to develop our purpose and capabilities, embracing all things and living for the good of all. Therefore, the spirit of Hongik has been more than a spiritual teaching; it's served as the principle of national education and as the governing ideology of Korea for thousands of years.

Long ago, I resolved to make Hongik—the spiritual root of Korean culture—the center of my own beliefs, philosophy, and vision. I thought of Hongik not as a dead word found only in history books but as the spirit most needed by the world today; it's the key to solving the challenges facing human society.

The Hongik spirit is the philosophical root of the Earth Citizen Movement, a pursuit I've been sharing with many people. With Hongik, it's not enough for my country alone to thrive. It's a spirit of coexistence that the world can share, seeking to work for the good of all people.

Coexistence is Hongik put into practice. To practice Hongik, we need great, bright wisdom, not just great love and purpose. The story of the troubled mother of two sons at the beginning of this chapter—the sandal-monger and the clog-monger—is more than a proverbial tale. It speaks of problems we experience daily in all areas of life. Suppose we're not talking about two individuals but about large groups, and those groups are entangled in conflicting interests. Where do we begin unraveling the knot of difficulties and confrontations between them?

The beginning of a solution is recognizing the right of coexistence for all the diversity in the world. Countless people exist in this world, people with different thoughts, different lifestyles, different skin colors, different tastes, and different political beliefs. Acknowledging they have a right to exist in this world the same as anyone—no more and no less—is the key to solving the problem.

It would be best to love your enemies and turn the other cheek, but going that far might not be easy. However, I can accept that other people have the same right to exist as I do, regardless of their skin color, nationality, or religious beliefs. Recognizing and respecting such rights is a basic responsibility for everyone with a conscience and common sense. Even this shift in our thinking could make the world much more peaceful, healthy, and sustainable. The history of evolution has consistently taught us that life without coexistence cannot last.

The fundamental cause of all conflicts on our planet is the failure to accept the coexistence of opposing values and beliefs. When I fail to recognize the coexistence of such contradictions, what's different from me becomes "evil"—something to be eliminated. Conflict and violence will overrun the world unless we accept the different, the antagonistic, the contradictory. This is true of all conflicts, including the opposition between North and South Korea, the antagonism between Israel and Palestine, and the competition for supremacy between China and the United States.

We must be able to resolve divisions, conflicts, and contradictions through peaceful coexistence rather than through the face-to-face showdowns that hurt winners and losers alike. The kind of divisive leadership that creates enemies to rally support for itself cannot bring about the changes the earth and humanity need today. We must drop the foolish idea that we can change the world—that we can save it—only by fighting and beating people who hold views opposite our own. With such outdated concepts, we see differences only as irreconcilable contradictions and know no way to overcome them other than by vanquishing each other. We need the tolerance, flexibility, and wisdom to accept the coexistence of contradictions.

When we accept the coexistence of contradictions, ours becomes a world where apparently contradictory things can exist together—an open world where we acknowledge and appreciate others. We shouldn't underestimate our brains' capacity. They have the capability to accommodate and reconcile seemingly incompatible values and phenomena. Far from being situations in which we must defeat the other side to win, contradictions are challenges and opportunities leading us to seek wiser answers—answers that benefit all.

CHAPTER 6

The Earth as the Central Value

"The world is my country, all mankind are my brethren, and to do good is my religion."

— Thomas Paine

In recent years, there have been numerous articles in the media about space exploration. While space travel in the past was led by national governments, the active participation of private companies has produced tangible results. Though limited to a small number of celebrities and the wealthy, space tourism programs for civilians have already been started on a trial basis. There is even talk of an era in which, in addition to mining resources in space, there will be "made in space" merchandise produced by 3D printers or robots and brought to Earth.

The space age certainly offers new possibilities for humankind and inspires new dreams. It might lead not only to exploring and pioneering outer space but also to discovering and interacting with other intelligent life forms or civilizations. Furthermore, it could mean humanity becoming part of a cosmic community larger than just the earth. These are amazing possibilities that could radically expand human consciousness and activities. But we need to resolve the relationship we currently have with the earth before that happens.

I Am from Earth

Just a few years ago, the opportunity for personal travel in space was nothing more than a fantasy. However, the development of new technologies focused on private space exploration has drastically reduced costs and risks, and now it is a feasible possibility within the lifetime of the current generation of humans. You and I might even have a chance to travel in space.

Imagine you went on a space voyage and had to make an emergency landing on another planet. Let's say there happened to be a form of intelligent life different from ours, and a member of that life form approached you with friendly interest. Would it ask about your name, your job, your age, or your gender? Probably not. That being would likely first ask, "Where are you from?" What would be your reply? Would you say that you are from the United States or Canada or China or Korea, or some other country? Would you tell them your ethnicity?

I'm sure you know that those answers wouldn't be helpful. A reasonable answer to the question, "Where are you from?" would be, "I am from Earth." The fact that we are from the earth—that we are Earth Citizens—is not artificial information, such as the names of countries, religions, or cultures. This is information given to us from the universe and from nature, and it would be valid no matter where we went in the universe, no matter how far and deep.

For too long, we have turned a blind eye to the self-evident fact that Earth Citizenship forms the very foundation of our identity. We've locked ourselves inside the boundaries of nationality, ethnicity, religion, and ideology. We've also rejected, excluded, and ravaged people with different belief systems or identities from our own.

Our current way of life is already that of Earth Citizens. How we communicate with each other and run businesses shows that we are Earth Citizens. The sense of identity that makes people limit themselves to a particular country, heritage, or religion is merely a stubborn habit and memory of a less-connected time that holds us back from keeping up with the changes of the real everyday world.

So, becoming an Earth Citizen is marked by a shift from whom we *think* we are to who we truly are. This isn't possible because of today's level of technology. It's because, from the beginning, there has only been one Earth. All other boundaries are artificial and exist only for convenience, and they are already falling apart from changes occurring every day. The fact that we are Earth Citizens is not a fantastical ideal; it's our concrete reality.

There is nothing that we need to learn and prepare to become Earth Citizens. We need only face the fact that our sense of identity, and the belief systems that sustained it until now, no longer fit the situation. We need to make the choice to shed the external layer of that information as though discarding clothes that our bodies have outgrown.

Think about how you felt when you could no longer wear your childhood clothes. During childhood, they had protected you from the cold wind and the hot sun so that you could grow safely. The days when you lived in those clothes will always remain a pleasant memory. It's just that you don't need them anymore now that you've outgrown them. Insisting on wearing those clothes would be strange. In the same way, becoming an Earth Citizen doesn't involve abandoning anything or becoming something new. It's about being who we are now.

When we truly accept that we are Earth Citizens, differences are no longer cause for conflict. Differences in culture, race, religion, and beliefs will be understood as diversity in coexistence. These differences need not be the seeds of dissension but a way of creating greater inclusion and abundance in the culture of humankind.

A Shared Scale for All Values

One legendary figure in nineteenth-century Korea is known for selling water from a big river. At the time, it didn't make sense to sell free-flowing water. People thought he was either a remarkable go-getter or a con artist, depending on their perspective. Nowadays, it's become odd *not* to pay for drinking water; we accept putting a price on food or water as a matter of routine. But what would happen if a price were put on the air we breathe? Through this last pandemic, we saw the possibility of something like that becoming a reality. What would you do if the amount of air you could breathe safely were limited? Only then would we realize the preciousness and value of the clean air we now breathe for free.

Currently, we use "the market" as a device for determining relative differences in value. Under this system, the value of a commodity fluctuates according to the balance of supply and demand for that item. A fatal flaw in this seemingly reasonable system is that it does not express with a price the values that aren't traded on the market—like clean water and clean air—but are genuinely essential for sustaining life.

What is the price of our one and only Earth, and the ecosystems of the earth that we have no idea how to restore once they collapse? When they have become damaged, who will pay the fee to restore them? Would that restoration even be possible? Our current market system is neither mature enough to include those values nor honest enough to acknowledge them, nor is it sensitive enough to address them.

Value systems influence more than the price of goods or services traded on the market. They affect every choice we make in our daily lives. Even in a single day, we need to make many choices. We can't choose everything we want, so we prioritize what's most important. Consciously or unconsciously, we each apply our own standard of values. The standard that I apply could be based on my personal interests or the interests of the group to which I belong, ranging from my family to my country, or perhaps my religious beliefs.

The numerous conflicts we are witnessing on the earth at present are clashes between such different value systems. The sharpest conflict arises when people try to impose their own value system upon others. Success, happiness, patriotism, religious faith—all such values are relative, as is shown by such conflicts. It might be more inclusive, and helpful for achieving peace, to acknowledge the relativity of values and let one another be, rather than insisting that one's own values are absolute. Yet, if we only try to avoid confrontation or intrusion into each other's domains, it will be difficult to respond to great challenges that can't be handled individually or to achieve great goals to help the collective whole.

Therefore, it would be hugely helpful to have a central value that everyone with common sense could accept. Other values pursued by individuals and groups could then be adjusted based on this central value. Determining priorities would reduce conflict and help with decision-making. And attributing relative value to objects of transaction based on this central value would make it possible to use resources and operate economic systems more efficiently.

What is the central value that could harmonize all the values in the world and promote mutual understanding and coexistence? I believe that value is the earth itself. The earth is not just a lump of land that we've been given for our feet to stand on. The earth is the foundation of all the values we seek. It is the root of our lives, the vital force of life itself within us.

Any value or truth that we seek can only be established on the premise of the earth's existence. Only the earth as our central value can bring all human consciousness together as one. All human activity for seeking value takes place on the earth. That makes the earth the value of all values, the fundamental value, the center of all values—not only for humans but for all life on the planet. The earth is not an ideal or an ideology, like peace or democracy, but an actual entity. Ideologies can be newly created, but if we lose this real and tangible value, there is no way we can get it back.

Why haven't we been able to properly understand the earth as a central and absolute value before now? That's likely because the earth is so big compared to the scale of what humans can recognize and experience. Like a fish swimming in the sea, unaware that the water even exists, we don't feel the presence of the earth because it is so enormous and so close. Fish competing for food see only the food in front of them as their life source. The great ocean where they live and, like us, the entire planet is the foundation of their life, but it's so massive and all-encompassing that they don't even feel its existence.

When you apply the standard of the earth as the central value, things that are good for me but not for other people are ultimately not good for me, either. Something that seems good for me and for other people, but is not good for the earth, is ultimately not good for me or for other people. So, whatever is good for me and other people while also good for the planet is good for everyone.

If you follow these standards and listen to the voice of conscience—the absolute truthfulness within us—and you follow the guidance of compassion, which feels the pain of others as no different from your own pain, you will surely be able to make wise choices that benefit all. I believe this is the most basic rule of life for creating a world of coexistence, a future where we live in harmony with all living beings.

This shift in perception is the most important key to a peaceful and sustainable world. When we properly understand the existence and meaning of the earth, the religion or country that we held to be an absolute value becomes a relative value.

The numerous disputes that have stained human history can be said to be the result of competition between relative values vying to reach the status of absolute value. Conflict was inevitable. Even if the claim was for the value of peace, the result was the same. Peace centered on one religion or one country is bound to result in conflict. Only when we recognize the earth as a central value, and when all religions, ideologies, and countries respect one another, acknowledging the relative value of each, can we lay the groundwork for true peace and open our minds to a sustainable future.

What Is the Earth to You?

What is the earth to you? Is it a disposable product to use as much as possible before throwing it away? There are people who argue that we need to pioneer other planets before the earth's environment becomes uninhabitable because of climate change and other crisis situations. The earth is obviously in a difficult situation right now, but it's not at a point where we should give up. We must pull together all our wisdom, capabilities, and resources to heal the wounds we've inflicted on the earth. Humanity has the capabilities and resources to do so. What we lack at present is trust in each other to make that kind of effort.

Even if we were to migrate to a new planet, if we then repeated the same behavior we'd exhibited on Earth, would our multi-planet civilization be sustainable? If we were to meet alien civilizations and join an alliance larger than that of Earth, with what status would we want to participate—as refugees who barely managed to escape a destroyed planet Earth or as proud members of the earth community who came together in solidarity to overcome challenges and achieve a mature, harmonious, and abundant civilization?

When human beings first appeared on Earth—a monkey-like life form intelligent enough to be aware of its own existence and feel reverence and curiosity about its source—it would have been natural for them to conclude that the earth is central to the workings of the universe and that they are the most important life form on the planet. But now we see a bigger picture, and it is proof that we have grown.

How humiliating it may have been to once think the earth is the center of the universe and then later to have to accept that it is not? It's time once again to face such a profound shift in perspective with humility. We need to demonstrate that our awareness has deepened and our point of view widened. A shift in perception equal to the Copernican shift must now happen again if we are to pull together to create a sustainable future.

The shift in perception that we need right now is to acknowledge that humans are not the center of the earth, and to find the central point required for coexistence. That central point is the earth itself. The criterion for assessing value is not one's personality, preconceptions, ideology, religion, or ethnicity, but the earth. This should be the basis for evaluation in all our activities. We are Earth Citizens before we are members of any country, ethnicity, or religion. Before we are American, Chinese, Korean, or Indian, and before we are Christian, Buddhist, Muslim, or Jewish, we are Earth Citizens.

CHAPTER 7

Managing the Earth Together

*"I thought I couldn't make a difference
because I was too small."*

— Greta Thunburg

Only a century ago, the average person considered their country the largest social unit they were part of. There was almost no need for ordinary people to think of the whole earth. But now everything has changed. The reach of our lives has expanded to encompass the entire world. However, our consciousness is still trapped in old worldviews. Such narrow viewpoints stand in the way of the world becoming a global village.

Since the critical problems confronting humanity now affect all nations, they can't be solved by the efforts of just a few specific groups or countries. Instead, we all need to work together and expand our focus. We need to shift our thinking from managing only our own communities and countries to managing the entire earth.

We normally see the earth as massive, identifying the planet with nature, calling it "mother" or "goddess," and even giving it mystical significance. So, the idea of "managing" the earth may not only seem strange but also feel grandiose or even dangerous to some.

The cosmos is still a mystery for our species, living as we do on one tiny planet among many orbiting the sun, which in turn is but one of countless stars in the Milky Way, which is one of approximately two trillion galaxies in the universe. In that sense, nature—the universe—remains vast and mysterious to us. When it comes to the earth, though, humankind now has the power to change the landscape, change the climate, change the ecosystem, and determine the planet's fate. We may call her "Mother Nature," but we cannot take from her like thoughtless, selfish children forever. We need to protect, manage, and take responsibility for our home like adults.

Can the Earth Be Managed?

What would happen if we thought of the earth as our land, home, and business, as if it were something we should take responsibility for, maintain, and manage? What choices and actions would we take if we viewed the present global situation with this attitude?

We cherish and take care of our homes and our land—tiny pieces of the earth's surface—as if we were going to be there for thousands of years. We're not much interested, though, in the planet itself, the very foundation of our land. Even business managers with integrity and responsibility, people trying to minimize waste and cost and optimize their activities, do not view planet-wide losses and expenses the same way they see their company finances.

We treat the earth like unmanaged public toilets. Everybody has the right to use the facilities, but nobody feels responsible for cleaning them. Obviously, such facilities become filthy in no time. That comes back to bite everyone who's using them.

As individuals, we're always involved in some form of management—from managing ourselves or our families to running a company or even a country. Earth Management is no different, except that the goals and values pursued are centered on the earth.

It's not uncommon for the interests of individuals to be sacrificed or compromised for the sake of higher values and the common good. We consider it a virtue of mature citizenship to prioritize community values if they collide with our individual values. When a nation is in crisis, it is natural for companies or organizations to transcend their narrow interests and cooperate for the country's well-being. When there is an apparent conflict between national and corporate interests, companies prioritizing their own interests are criticized as irresponsible or unscrupulous.

However, we are not yet applying these same standards to the planet. Earth is at the very top of the multilevel community to which we belong. It is our most comprehensive community, including humans and all living things. Earth Management recognizes the planet as our ultimate community and prioritizes the earth over the interests of any individual, group, or nation.

Management is a familiar word in business, leading some people to think of a globalized business when they hear the expression "Earth Management." How is Earth Management different from the globalization of business? The fundamental difference lies in the goals that are involved. Business globalization seeks to increase dominance and maximize profits by expanding markets and supply chains worldwide. The goal of Earth Management, on the other hand, is coexistence. It's about everyone living together— not about any individuals, organizations, or countries winning a competition so they can rule over other people, organizations, or countries.

Earth Management is about everyone managing and caring for the planet, with the earth itself as the central value and coexistence as the goal. This is something that's beyond the capabilities of any individual, nation, or specific system. Everyone living on the planet shares in the responsibility. Anyone managing their own life by placing the earth at the center of their value judgments participates in Earth Management, no matter where they are on the planet.

Earth Management Scenario

What form should Earth Management take? The most easily conceivable possibility is that of a loose system of coordination organized through an international consultative body such as the United Nations.

It has been 76 years since the creation of the United Nations (UN). The UN has carried out many activities during that time, and South Korea, in particular, was one of the most direct beneficiaries. The Korean War was the first and last time the UN intervened directly in a war under the United Nations Command (UNC). Since then, the UN has never tried to resolve a dispute by organizing military forces under the UNC, although it has provided peacekeepers and restoration support in the aftermath of war.

A frequently-cited limitation of international organizations such as the UN is that their procedures are so complex, time-consuming, and inefficient that it can take months to revise a single phrase of an agreement. This problem is unavoidable for an organization that collects and coordinates the opinions of countries with differing interests. In some cases, a situation may already have changed by the time an agreement is completed.

Another limitation of the UN is the influence of the permanent members of the Security Council and other powerful countries, especially the United States and China in the present day. In 2020, US President Donald Trump announced that the United States would withdraw from the World Health Organization and stop supporting it because he considered it biased toward China.

Although the United States annulled this policy as soon as a new administration took office, it showed that international organizations are less powerful than we'd thought. Lacking financial capacity and relying on contributions and subsidies from participating nations—especially economically powerful countries—the United Nations is not free from their influence.

Consequently, it is sometimes criticized for acting as a mere spokesperson for the great powers, rubber-stamping and justifying their decisions. International organizations such as the United Nations play a coordinating role and are still needed, but we can hardly expect them to perform more than their current functions. Despite the efforts of the United Nations, local conflicts and hegemonic competition continue, and the global environment changes daily, approaching a point of no return.

A system of consolidated, monopolistic control like that seen in the world economy is another possibility for Earth Management. Consolidation on a global scale has been steady in industry, where top competitors have been reduced to four or five companies in major industries such as energy, grain, aircraft, pharmaceuticals, and automobiles. And if an industry has only one supplier, it will operate differently than it would if it faced competition. An economy dominated by inter-industry consolidation can no longer be called a capitalist market economy. Monopolization of capital and technology, and the control that brings, is happening worldwide. Here we should ask about the difference between domination and management.

Imagine a situation where beings more evolved than humans debate Earth's and humanity's future. "Humans are rough, short-sighted, and egotistical," those wanting more complete control might argue. "If left to their own devices, they'll destroy themselves and their environment. Let's create a good framework and have them live within it; otherwise, the planet is doomed. If we put things off, there may be no going back, and we may have to make them disappear to preserve the planet the way we did with the dinosaurs."

It's an imaginary story, of course, but do you have any counterarguments? Though we can see the global crisis with our own eyes, we don't want to sacrifice even trivial personal conveniences or profit for the earth's sake. Global agreements for saving the planet are discarded in favor of short-term national interests or political popularity. That's the reality we face. It's also our reality that politicians are pouring resources into war and an arms race, putting us on the road to self-destruction.

The apparent human drive to dominate often over-shadows our ability to manage. Management is about individuals exercising their capabilities and harmoniously organizing that power to reach a common goal. In contrast, domination unilaterally sets and enforces the rules, considering only efficiency and results rather than the spontaneity and creativity of individuals. If the essence of humanity is selfish existence trapped within the limits of the ego, then we are destined to let the few who monopolize capital and technology dominate us.

It would be bleak if these were the only possibilities before us, but fortunately, there is another way: the path of voluntary solidarity by people who share common sense, responsibility, and hope. Grandiose enlightenment isn't necessary for participating in Earth Management. What's needed is a common-sense understanding that coexistence is better than mutual destruction. This mindset accepts that the future of our species is our choice and responsibility, no one else's; it's a mindset that chooses hope.

I've seen the power of this perspective in many people. I've seen it through my own life and in the upright, kind, bright hearts of many people I've met. On countless occasions, I've witnessed how great changes can occur once people start using the power of their minds. And I know with certainty that this bright mindset and great love exist in everyone.

We can trust and connect with others based on this mindset within ourselves. Security systems ultimately can't tell us how safe and healthy our society is. Rather, it's how many people have this mindset and are connected to one another on this basis. Earth's future depends on how many people accept saving the earth as their own problem, take responsibility for it, and act on it. Fortunately, technology is now in place to allow us to connect with each other and exercise the power of collective choice across regional, political, and cultural boundaries.

With this understanding, we can escape from the thought that Earth Management is too big or irrelevant for us as individuals. Earth Management may sound grandiose, but in fact, it should be common sense for everyone living in these times. Like-minded people amplify the power of choice and action by connecting, exchanging information, and cooperating rather than trying to go it alone.

Our Individual Choices Change the World

An image that might come to mind when you think about the dangers of climate change is that of a mother polar bear floating on a piece of ice, anxious for her young cubs. Or you might envision trees in a tropical forest cut down and rolling on the ground. The emotional appeal of such images gives us the feeling that we should do something on polar ice caps or in the rainforests to make a change.

But it's not what's happening in the Arctic that is melting the ice there. Rainforests aren't just cut down for the people who live there. The place where change must happen to protect the polar bears and preserve the rainforests is where each of us is right now. Many things can change if we just remember the planet and consider it when making our everyday choices, such as keeping indoor temperatures appropriate, choosing drought-resistant landscaping, and consciously considering what food we order and what necessities we decide to buy.

One example illustrating the power of our choices is the growth of the organic food business. Organic food is currently one of the fastest-growing segments of the food industry in the world. It was already a while ago that Walmart became the largest organic food vendor in the United States, though it had once seemed the least likely store to sell organic products. Within just two years, the world's largest distributor found new suppliers and set up a distribution network.

How were such rapid changes possible? What made this possible was the power of consumer choice. No business in the world is free from consumer decisions. Businesses develop, change, adjust production, or discontinue products depending on consumer choices. Remember—you're voting every time your barcode is read at a checkout counter and every time you click the buy button online. Companies change their products and behaviors based on these votes.

Walmart became the largest seller of organic food because of the power of consumer choice, not because of its CEO's special love for the earth. If purely voluntary and individual consumer choices can change the world's top retailer in two years, there is no business or organization that cannot be changed this way. By exercising their power of choice more consciously and systematically, consumers can transform businesses and organizations, countries, and even the whole world.

We are the first generation in human history able to change the world through our individual choices. Previously, personal decisions didn't have enough impact to change the state of the planet. For example, a century ago it didn't make much difference whether you recycled or what your dietary choices were. Now, though, the situation has changed. Over the past 100 years, the global population has quadrupled, growing from two billion to eight billion. The rate of environmental pollution and ecosystem destruction caused by human activities is accelerating. One person's choices may seem weak and ineffectual, but as our ability to communicate and connect with one another grows, our individual choices matter much more. We all can—and already do—participate in Earth Management through our personal choices.

A Sustainable *and* Prosperous Life Is Possible

Are sustainability and abundant living incompatible goals? How can people's desire for a more prosperous life be met without an increase in material production and external economic growth? Many people think a sustainable environment and a growing economy are incompatible, and sometimes those who prioritize sustainability are accused of not understanding economics.

The essence of productive activity in an economy is creating value, not simply producing more goods. Value varies depending on what things we need and how we prioritize them. The environmental conditions that have made human survival possible haven't been thought of as economically valuable because in the past we believed them to be eternal. But aren't clean air and water more important than any advanced technology? If we assess the economic value of a clean environment, could a country with an abundance of expensive items but a ruined environment be called rich? Is a nation living simply but maintaining a clean environment poorer than a country enjoying non-sustainable material abundance?

Tear a piece of paper in two and then try to put the torn pieces back together. It takes more effort and dedication to restore something—even a piece of paper—than it does to tear it up. So far, development and economic growth have focused on destroying natural conditions to extract resources. But sustainable development focuses on restoration and healing.

As in the example of putting the ripped paper back together, this could create more jobs than environmentally damaging production does. If people need and value restoration, resources both from the private sector and governments will be redirected toward that because that's how the market system works. Money goes where people find value. It can also create value that's incomparably greater than any goods produced for consumption.

Many companies have voluntarily started to include the environmental impact of their production activities in their profit and loss calculations. Efforts are being made to evaluate the productivity of companies by considering their ecological footprints. Those who run businesses now recognize that strengthening their social responsibility and engaging in sustainable practices is an opportunity for business growth.

Another crucial thing to consider is the distinction between abundance and waste. For example, a third of all the food produced today is wasted without ever reaching consumers. And a significant amount of cooked food is thrown away by consumers as garbage. Yet, as of 2020, more than 800 million people worldwide are chronically malnourished. That constitutes 11 percent of the world's population. Food waste also has a significant impact on climate change. The United Nations Environment Programme estimates that 8 to 10 percent of global green-house gas emissions are caused by the loss and disposal of agricultural products. Reducing waste in food—and in life in general—dramatically helps to cut costs, protect the envi-ronment, and ensure that resources are recycled.

All these facts tell us that sustainability and abundant living are compatible. By centering our standards of value on the planet, prioritizing our economic activities to match these values, and reducing waste in our lives, we can create a life that is both sustainable and prosperous.

You Are That Person

Many of us may feel that what we do every day is insignifi-cant in the big picture. For instance, they may think, "What does cooking at home have to do with the earth?" But the seemingly trivial things we do each day are all related to the environment and the future of the planet. I'm cooking for

Earth Management. I'm teaching children for Earth Management. I'm cleaning for Earth Management. People change when they make up their minds to keep the big picture in their hearts. It isn't easy to feel the value of your work or life when you follow routines just to make a living. But whatever you're doing, wherever and with whomever you're doing it, all the activities in your life take on value when you think of them as contributing to Earth Management.

Empowering every individual to have love for other human beings, gratitude for the earth, and faith in humanity, and to act accordingly—that is the way of Earth Management. The path of coexistence and the dream of Earth Management that I envision will be realized not through rules or systems but by everyone following the guidance of conscience and the empathy within themselves, thereby achieving order and harmony for the good of all.

The way to coexistence and peace is not a path of fierce fighting but one of helping and healing each other. Coexistence and peace are both the goal and the process. By practicing coexistence, we achieve it, and by practicing peace, we realize it. Playing together, we heal one another. Look at the popular South Korean boy band BTS. They sing and dance with excitement, making people happy, giving them courage, healing their wounds, and expanding global pop culture.

It's enough for each of us to use the talents we have. We don't necessarily have to create an organization. It's like the army of fans who get together during a BTS performance, mingle with one another, send messages, and then go back to their own lives when the performance is over. It's enough to come and go freely, sharing the message of coexistence, spreading the Earth-Citizen lifestyle without becoming addicted to anything or excluding anyone. The important thing is to share honestly what you know and feel with those around you rather than keeping it to yourself, to sympathize with the messages of other like-minded people, and to cheer each other on.

You don't need to categorize your mindset or behavior according to standards like "left" or "right," "progressive" or "conservative." Instead, just follow your conscience and feelings of empathy, making choices that are good for you and good for the earth.

The one thing we must never do is to give up. We must go all the way with our dream of a beautiful world, a world where harmonious coexistence is a reality.

I dream of leaders who are firm but not stiff, serious but not heavy-handed or severe. I dream of leaders who are strong yet gentle, kind and innocent, yet wise. I want to see leaders with kind hearts who share in the pain and joy of others. I hope for leaders who know how to distinguish between their egos and their consciences and who will listen to the voice of their conscience when the two are at odds. I dream of leaders with a vision of saving the world, not the ambition to dominate it. With that leader in your heart, *you* are an Earth Manager.

PART 3

Suggestions for a Peaceful, Sustainable World

CHAPTER 8

Education that Teaches What's Important

*"Intelligence plus character—
that is the goal of true education."*

— Martin Luther King, Jr.

Around the start of the COVID pandemic, I was staying in Kerikeri, New Zealand, preparing for the development of Earth Village. I was focused on creating educational facilities where anyone could learn eco-friendly life skills and cultivate Earth Citizen consciousness. But in the early days of the pandemic, New Zealand implemented a nationwide lockdown more swiftly and more thoroughly than any other nation, leaving me stranded in the country. Plans for the development of Earth Village were suspended, along with the travel plans of people who had wanted to visit Earth Village to experience meditation. I had scheduled workshops and conferences in New Zealand and many other countries, but nothing could be carried out as planned.

When all the events were cancelled, I rolled up my sleeves and started working on developing an animal farm. I'd always thought about this, but I hadn't been able to devote enough time to make it happen. I worked outdoors every day with different members of the staff to build roads and fences, along with houses for the animals. One activity that I really enjoyed was caring for the farm animals. Our farm grew in scale as various animals—including cows, pigs, goats, and geese—had babies.

As I watched the babies grow, I was especially impressed by the animals' remarkable ability to adapt. Barely a few hours after being born, a calf gets up and starts to walk. There was one little piglet who was dying after eating a poisonous plant, but I did acupuncture and qigong massage and was able to save him. I named him Lucky, and in less than a year, he became a father pig.

Watching the animals' rapid growth and incredible ability to adapt made me feel, once again, the fragility of human survival conditions. Humans often can't stand on our own two feet for a year after being born. It may take one to two years to understand people's words and communicate basic expressions. Then humans typically enter an educational curriculum that may last 17 years or even more, starting with preschool and kindergarten and lasting through college and perhaps graduate school. It's not until about 18 years of age that we can make decisions for ourselves. The lives we will live after this period and the impact our lives will leave on the world will differ depending on the people we interact with, the information we accept, and the environment we're surrounded by during this developmental stage of our lives.

The long period of child-rearing is both a weakness and a great strength of humankind. As they develop, individuals have no choice but to rely on other members of their family and the larger community for food, clothing, safety, and education. If no one provides adequate protection and parenting, it is challenging to grow normally or even to survive. On the other hand, because there is such a long period of protection and child-rearing, it is possible to acquire, use, and further develop the vast array of cultural assets that humankind has accumulated—including the knowledge and skills necessary for living.

What society will look like in the future depends on what happens to children growing up today. While there may be many differences in individual experience, family and school generally have the most significant influence. A critical indicator of our future societal health is our current classroom environment since the minds that will create our future society are forming there.

The Classroom Landscape

I have heard about the current South Korean high school classroom situation from acquaintances with direct experience on campuses. They tell me that half the students in the class are sleeping, and two-thirds of those awake are paying attention to something other than schoolwork. Only about 10 percent are focusing on the class. Of course, this wouldn't describe all the high school classrooms in South Korea, and classroom environments in other countries could be different. But, the disparity between educational content and real life, combined with excessive competition, is becoming an issue in almost every country.

In an educational system with an intense focus on college admission, such as in South Korea, competition starts in elementary school. For 12 years, students spend their school time acquiring the information they'll need for college entrance examinations. That leaves neither educators nor students with the mental space to take an interest in the practical knowledge, skills, wisdom, or character necessary for truly successful living. If only 10 percent are focused on learning, what significance does school hold for the majority of students who already expected to fail? Before I saw this as a problem with the current functioning of schools, it was a question that I had had for a long time, based on my personal experience in my youth.

My teenage years weren't particularly happy. In fact, I was very depressed and pessimistic about everything. At the age when I should have been concentrating on my studies, my head was filled with fundamental doubts about life that others would have considered absurd. But I was drawn to these questions and couldn't focus on my classroom studies. When I took notes, I couldn't read my handwriting afterward, and eventually I didn't bother to take notes at all. Making up my mind to study and get into college happened only after I felt a sense of responsibility about my life and had a vague idea about the value of my existence.

I have felt great anguish for students who are suffering through adolescence in their school systems without having clear goals or hopes—like me back in my youth. The conviction I have gained by experiencing the infinite potential of the human brain has deepened this anguish. The latent potential and creativity of the brain are not developed by acquiring a lot of intellectual knowledge. I spent my years in school depressed and without any dreams, but after finding my personal dream, I could demonstrate creativity and accomplish my chosen goals.

I had long felt the need for a school that helps students discover their self-worth and dreams while teaching practical knowledge and skills to help them live responsible lives. I decided that if such a school didn't exist, I would create one myself. What I started is an alternative school called the Benjamin School for Character Education.

Benjamin School for Character Education

The name "Benjamin School" originates from Benjamin Franklin, a historical figure I like and respect. One of the United States founders, Benjamin Franklin was a politician who left an important mark on American history. He also made significant achievements in other areas, including publishing and science.

Benjamin Franklin was a man of great learning in many fields, though he only had two years of formal schooling. He then gained other knowledge and skills through self-study. Famously, he was so curious that he flew a kite on a stormy day to learn the nature of lightning. Through this experiment, he discovered that lightning was a function of electricity and invented the lightning rod—which prevents lightning-caused disasters. Franklin was a person of outstanding character as demonstrated through his spirit of experimentation and tireless effort for self-development, his practice of making his actions match his words to uphold the rules he set for himself, and his respect for knowledge and skills. These characteristics corresponded well with the values I intended for this new school I envisioned, so I included "Benjamin" in the school name.

There are five elements usually found at schools that the Benjamin School for Character Education does *not* have: classrooms, subject classes, homework assignments, tests, and grade reports. Many people would probably be puzzled upon hearing this, and they might ask, "Well, then, how is that a school?"

Instead of these five components, the Benjamin School incorporates a "Dream Project" that students plan and execute themselves. There is hands-on study for learning through real-life experiences, and there are mentors who help students through this process. As they carry out their Dream Projects over about a year, students learn to make choices for themselves and take responsibility for those choices. They realize that many people, including their parents, worked hard and took care of them so they could attend school, and they learn both modesty and gratitude. By discovering and choosing the goals they want to achieve in their lives, they have the passion and will for their self-development and growth.

So far, about 1,300 students have attended Benjamin School since it opened in 2014. They come from different backgrounds and have unique motivations for wanting to participate in the school. Depending on the Dream Projects they've chosen, their experiences at Benjamin School also vary. But they all have in common that by discovering their own value and choosing their individual goals, they become more proactive and responsible for their personal growth. These goals are the essence of education as I think of it. I have high hopes that every graduate of Benjamin School will continue to cultivate these values. I also hope that the example of Benjamin School will serve as a stimulus for working together to improve the current educational systems so more students can find their self-worth.

Education for Future Life

Most large companies, especially in technology-related industries, conduct professional development courses for new employees over one or two years. They say this updated, additional education is necessary because the knowledge and skills learned in university courses are too outdated to be applied in the field.

This situation doesn't apply only to universities. Curriculum changes come about even more slowly for elementary, middle, and high schools than for universities. And even if the content is updated, it's not easy to apply those changes without retraining the teachers who need to deliver the new content. Thus, many students attain practical understanding of the world through the Internet rather than through the school curriculum. This situation makes us question the value of traditional education and whether it helps students to live their future lives well.

I believe education needs to change to cultivate leaders who will create a peaceful and sustainable future for humankind in today's changing environment. If we want a peaceful, sustainable world, the fundamentals of compulsory education should include the following: development of a character that makes harmonious coexistence possible; establishment of healthy living habits, values, and life goals; cultivation of sensibility and responsibility toward the environment; and teaching of practical knowledge and skills for managing one's life responsibly.

Character for Coexistence

I believe character-building is the most crucial aspect of education for helping students live their future lives well. Thus, I included "character" in the Benjamin School name. The Korean word for "character," *inseong*, contains the characters for "human" and "original nature," or "the nature of being human." Our character then can be an expression of who we are, and as such, is the most fundamental factor affecting an individual's quality of life over a lifetime, playing a decisive role in determining that person's success in the long run. Everyone knows the importance of character, but our current educational system, family culture, and societal environment often lack the appropriate conditions for building character.

An interesting study on human beings' benevolent nature was conducted in 2010 at Yale University's Infant Cognition Center, with the results published in the science journal *Nature*. Researchers showed babies aged three to nine months a simple puppet show with triangular, square, and round wooden figures marked with eye-shaped black dots. In one scene, a red circle tries to climb a hill, but a yellow triangle pushes it down to prevent it from climbing. In another scene, a blue square pushes the red circle from behind to help it climb up the hill. Afterward, when the babies were offered those wood pieces, most chose the blue square.

In another puppet show, a cat doll played with two rabbit dolls wearing different-colored shirts. The rabbit in the orange shirt caught the ball when the cat threw it and then tossed it back to the cat. But when the ball was thrown to the rabbit in the green shirt, it immediately ran away with it. When the babies were shown the two rabbit dolls afterward, they all chose the one with the orange shirt. Said the head researcher, "It seems that the ability to distinguish between bad and good people is something we're born with."

These infants hadn't yet learned what is good or what is evil, and they didn't yet have the intellectual ability or linguistic proficiency to understand ethical concepts. So how were they able to consistently demonstrate such a clear preference for kindness and prosocial behavior? The babies most likely made their choices not through intellectual understanding but through the feelings in their brains. Just as children laugh when sensations feel good and cry over unpleasant sensations, perhaps they instinctively have the feeling of being helped and accepted as well as the feeling of being blocked and rejected.

Many studies show that empathy and a benevolent character are innate to the human brain. This shows great potential for the creation of a more inclusive and compassionate world. It certainly gives us hope, along with a heavy responsibility. What kind of brain is the product of our current educational systems? Are we cultivating beautiful brains that help, are kind to one another, and like to play together—or are we nipping all of that in the bud?

Character education starts with the belief that since essential human nature has the characteristics of benevolence and kindness, helping people cultivate these qualities leads to desirable character. Injecting information without moving the heart, making evaluations based on competition, or attempting character development through force produces the opposite of real character education.

A Healthy Lifestyle

A second aspect that education needs to emphasize is healthy living habits. Adults are aware of how habits take root little by little without their realizing it, and how once rooted, they are hard to change. Some people have succeeded in changing unwanted habits through tremendous will and effort. But many more spend their whole lives rebuking themselves for being unable to break free from the hamster wheel of their habits, or they give up on changing and assume this is a burden they'll have to carry throughout their lives.

Eating habits are among the most basic and important of habits. The United States currently has the highest rates of obesity and diabetes worldwide. Obesity as an important national health issue in the US is not a recent development, but a new issue is the rapid increase in childhood obesity and diabetes—and similar situations are arising in countries around the world. South Korea is no exception to the increase in childhood obesity. Despite healthy eating habits being so important, almost no schools make them an educational goal.

The same goes for exercise. Regardless of race, nationality, or culture, no other habits affect our lifetime health as much as eating and exercise. Thanks to having physical training ingrained in me as I practiced Taekwondo in my youth, I move my body and exercise every chance I get. I am grateful for having acquired this habit when I was young. Exercise not only helps maintain physical strength and vitality, it also plays an important role in maintaining brain health by preventing depression and dementia, warding off the aging of brain cells, and aiding in the production of new brain cells. Exercise doesn't simply help you have an attractive body in your youth; it is an essential element of lifelong health.

Aside from diet and exercise, other important habits, such as proper posture and breathing, affect the health of the body and the brain throughout one's lifetime. Helping students grasp the right habits through their educational curricula would be a much greater help to them than a piece of intellectual information they'll soon forget.

Life Values and Goals

The most important thing in education is guiding people to realize their self-worth and to choose their life goals. As I've watched Benjamin School students go through the process of growth, I've felt that the reason many teenagers struggle with school isn't that studying is difficult. It's that they don't fully understand why they have to study at all. No matter how great a goal parents or school teachers may present, it is useless if students don't feel it in their hearts. When students choose a goal and find motivation, nobody can do it for them. They have to do it themselves or it will not be genuine.

Students at Benjamin School plan and carry out projects to develop their abilities and make positive contributions to society. Most of them look for projects in areas where they already have interest. As they work on their projects, they see and experience how they can affect other people's lives and their communities.

The most important part of this experience isn't words of praise from others but the feeling of recognition, love, and encouragement that comes from their inner selves. This feeling is unlike the sense of superiority or achievement that people may feel by beating others in a competition or doing well on a test. The words and actions of others can convey recognition, love, and encouragement, but self-satisfaction resonates much more deeply. The being that creates that feeling is not the personal self one usually knows but a being of much greater depth, benevolence, maturity, and thoughtfulness.

The self-recognition conveyed by such feelings is more powerful and persuasive than anyone else's words. As you accept that feeling and get closer to it, you begin to know that your true value is absolute, unaffected by external conditions such as your appearance, grades, or finances. You realize that you truly love the world and want to benefit it widely. And, you choose a goal for your life through which you can actualize such a noble desire. While striving to realize your chosen goal, all the abilities your brain possesses are developed and expressed, and you grow into a competent leader, not just a good-natured person. I've experienced this in my own life, and I've seen it in many other people working to achieve the visions that they have.

Sensibility and Responsibility Toward the Earth

Earth sensibility (mentioned in Chapter 4) refers to a deep emotional connection with the earth and the natural environment. It means feeling yourself as part of nature and accepting the earth as part of yourself. Through this sense, we develop a caring mindset toward the earth, loving it like our own bodies, homes, or gardens.

The most effective way to develop earth sensibility is to start at an early age. We must guide children to awaken and develop this sense at home and school. It is beneficial to allow many opportunities to encounter and interact with nature. You don't have to go out of your way to find a grand tourist attraction or a spectacular landscape. Vista-based sightseeing—where you look at nature from a distance— doesn't help much. But it's perfectly possible to interact with nature at a local park, a nearby mountain, or even through your home landscaping, a vegetable garden, or a nearby farm.

There are many excellent forms of experiential education for children: observing trees or flowers blooming and wilting with the seasons and recognizing their names; digging and touching the soil with your hands and looking at whatever creatures may live there; planting, cultivating, and harvesting vegetables and flowers; and cooking things you've harvested and eating them as you share your experiences. Such experiences also create opportunities for people to communicate more closely and comfortably as they work together. Education that fosters familiarity with nature can be even more effective in tandem with education about how our consumption of resources and energy impacts the earth, along with specific practices for a sustainable planet.

A middle school environmental educator once shared some interesting observations in a newspaper. Most of his students had lived in apartments since birth, riding in cars to go anywhere and living daily lives consisting of nothing but traveling between school and home. They had almost no opportunities to come in contact with nature up close. He took his students to a forest near the school and regularly made time for them to take pictures of trees and flowers and observe the ecology. He was shocked that it wasn't until they had this experience as teenagers that some of his students felt trees were living things like themselves.

Earth sensibility needs to be an essential teaching, just like basic moral principles like "don't lie," "don't take things that belong to other people," and "get along with your friends." What if we were to teach our children early on to feel and protect the natural environment as if it were their own bodies? With such guidance in childhood, they would grow into mature Earth Citizens who practice responsibility toward the earth. More than rules or coercion, earth sensibility and internalized behavior guidelines can guide us to live healthier and more sustainable lifestyles.

Practical Knowledge and Skills for a Responsible Life

Education also needs to include practical knowledge and skills to help people run their lives responsibly. This curriculum could include managing money, sex, emotions, communication, farming, cooking, and self-healing methods.

What are the basic things people need to manage to live as mature and responsible adults? I believe the three most crucial adult concerns are money, sex, and emotions. Many people manage these poorly, even as they get older. As a result, they hurt not only themselves but others as well.

How did *you* learn about money and sex? What feelings remain from that process? Many people know about these two things through experiences of lack, failure, and hurt—primarily alone or in conversations with peers who have similar levels of experience. Of course, we cannot eliminate failure and hurt in life; such experiences can make us stronger and more careful. But receiving wise and thoughtful mentoring in an open and inclusive environment would help students reflect on their personal experiences in a more balanced way.

Education about finances should include the value of work as a way of making money, social responsibility regarding earning and spending money, and saving and investing as ways to manage and put money to use. Many statistics show significant differences in later economic stability between students who learn these concepts early on and those who do not. As one educational policy related to money, for example, we could consider giving a certain amount of money to students when they graduate from high school to help them start their lives as adults. First of all, this could be an incentive for completing high school. And providing the money in the form of an investment account instead of cash would be a wonderful gift for becoming an adult, one that could let them learn how to manage money responsibly.

Being able to regulate emotions and communicate thoughts coherently without hurting another person's feelings are also essential skills that come in handy anytime and anywhere, even as an adult. In many areas of society, the factors that determine success in the long run aren't things like knowledge or certification but the ability to empathize and communicate. These are traits that enable people to work harmoniously with others.

Cooking and farming are also basic skills, but the purpose of learning them isn't to become a professional chef or an expert farmer. It's so that people know how the foods they eat are grown and prepared and have the minimum knowledge and capabilities necessary to prepare and manage their food. Such skills are of great help in managing one's health and reducing personal expenses, and they contribute to creating a sustainable planet.

We've grown accustomed to looking to pharmacies and doctors for even minor health problems. That's why it feels unfamiliar to take charge of our own health and to deal with symptoms on our own. But our bodies have an amazing ability to heal themselves, so many symptoms can be improved with just a little bit of care and help on our part. Such healing methods include breathing techniques, yoga, qigong, acupuncture, moxibustion, and acupressure. Of course, practices such as acupuncture or qigong require specialized knowledge and a long training period. But acupressure or moxibustion can be learned and practiced on your own without difficulty.

All these skills are easy to learn, interesting, and practical. They can be used and adapted to any living condition, wherever you might go. In learning such skills, your understanding of the body and mind deepens, and your understanding, consideration, patience, and love for the world and human beings become greater.

Education for Using Your Brain Effectively

We live in an era in which finding knowledge is easy with a mobile phone, anytime and anywhere. This fact doesn't mean that learning things is unnecessary. There's a difference between having knowledge in my brain that I can access and apply to a situation as necessary and constantly having to search for the information I need. For example, memorizing the multiplication table means I can use it at any time versus pulling out a chart or calculator whenever I need to do a calculation. Knowledge itself opens up a new understanding and perspective of the world. In acquiring knowledge such as mathematics or logic, for example, our thinking and judgment can become more lucid and better articulated.

Is the intellectual knowledge currently being taught helping students develop these qualities of the mind? In reality, these capacities develop more efficiently by overcoming real-life challenges than by memorizing textbook information. In trying to improve the environment in her city, one student at Benjamin School attained abundant and practical knowledge, from the nature of environmental problems to the ways we might solve these problems. Another student developed an expert-level understanding of fluid dynamics, aerodynamics, electricity, and engineering while studying to obtain a drone pilot license.

Through their various digital devices, youth are already living in an environment influenced by the culture of not just one country but almost everywhere in the world. Members of today's younger generation have grown and developed on a foundation that enables them to become Earth Citizens, becoming more sensitive than any other generation to the values of connection, sharing, respect for diversity and individuality, and sustainability.

Previous generations may have the impression that millennials and Gen Z members lack patience or consistency, are selfish, have poor manners, and don't have a sense of belonging or loyalty. But these characteristics can represent freedom from the existing value systems; a fluid sense of belonging that comes together or falls apart according to sentiments, tastes, and mindsets rather than regions or blood ties; and respect and honesty about feelings. Although inexperience may cause some clumsiness, this mindset realizes the characteristics required by citizens of a truly global community in the future. Perhaps these are qualities that older generations should learn from the millennials and Gen Z.

Because of millennials and Gen Z characteristics, old educational methods that unilaterally deliver information and enforce rules often fail. The most effective teaching method I could confirm through my experience with Benjamin School was to help students choose Dream Projects that suit their own goals and interests and support them with mentoring as they carry out their projects.

Students plan and implement their projects themselves, running into reality in the process. They receive mentoring from experts well-versed in the field, but the students themselves are responsible for completing their projects from beginning to end. Through this process, they develop practical knowledge, skills, confidence, responsibility, and leadership that they could not attain simply by reading a few books.

This approach to education is ultimately about believing in the human brain and its bright wisdom and helping students find and nurture it in themselves. In *Samilshingo*, one of the Korean people's oldest scriptures, there is a phrase that expresses the true value of the brain. It reads, "Each person must seek their own divine nature," and "It is already descended in your brain." These statements mean that the mind that is ever so bright, with conscience and empathy, is already in each person's brain.

I have created and shared Brain Education based on this understanding and belief in the brain and the human mind. Restoring and cultivating character, conscience, and creativity is what I aim to achieve through Brain Education. Once individuals select a goal on this basis and the motivation is clear, they can acquire the necessary knowledge and skills much more quickly. I believe that in this way, education can be a powerful mechanism contributing to the realization of a world of harmonious coexistence.

CHAPTER 9

Going beyond Success toward Completion

"Do not seek death. Death will find you.
But seek the road which makes death a fulfillment."

— Dag Hammarskjold

The mind able to manifest coexistence is the mind that wants things to work out well for everyone. All people wish things will work out for themselves or their children, but not everyone has a mindset that wishes *everybody* well. Of course, we all have the seed of such a mindset, but it's not fully grown in every person.

When there's something available to eat, a young child who doesn't know better will put it in their mouth, whatever it may be. But if a hungry baby were to give its food to other people, rather than marveling at this kind-heartedness, we would probably feel that the child's health should be checked. People gradually become more considerate of others as they grow older, but when you're young, people likely won't look down on you for seeing the world from a self-centered perspective or behaving as though everyone is looking at you. When you become an adult, have a family, and make a home, it gradually becomes second nature to take care of other people and be considerate of them. But even then, for most people, their own family takes priority.

The desire for things to work out well for everyone blossoms with old age. That mindset comes alive and grows deeper when the kids are grown up and independent, and one no longer has to struggle so much to take care of oneself. Of course, age itself doesn't bring you that mentality—it is a gift that life gives to people who have upright character and have worked hard to do their best so there's not much to regret.

As we get older, there is decreased secretion of hormones that stimulate aggression and sexual desire, such as adrenaline and testosterone, and an increase in the production of oxytocin, which promotes bonding, trust, and consideration toward others. The resulting changes in the brain, combined with decades of life experience, form the mentality of wishing for things to work out well for everyone. In such a perspective, the experiences of failure from days past aren't just memories of regret or pain. Rather, they manifest as tolerance for other people's mistakes, understanding and encouragement for people in despair, and support for taking on challenges. We come to have a mindset of patience and thoughtfulness toward both those of our own blood and many people around us—a grandparents' mindset.

Often when disputes arise between people, the elderly can act as mediators. The outlook that naturally develops with old age helps make good decisions without bias. It's not any special knowledge or spiritual awakening that becomes a source of wisdom and a valuable factor in creating a culture of harmonious coexistence, but the mind that wishes for *everyone* to have good fortune and prosper.

Are You Ready for a Long Life?

As of 2020, the average life expectancy of Americans was 77 years. Young adults now 20–30 years old may live past age 100 regularly, and children born now may even live past the age of 120. The era of the 100-year lifetime has become a common-sense concept not just in a few countries but globally. Biological life expectancy has increased through improved quality of life and advances in medical technology, but how are we prepared—personally and as a society—for this period of longevity?

The biggest problem is the sudden cessation of productive activities after age 65. Right now, we live in a societal system where most social contributions happen between the ages of 20 and 65. If people retire and cease their career activities at around 65, they will likely be left with at least 20 more years of life, possibly even 40 years. Those with sufficient economic means to carry them through that time are in the minority; most people have to make ends meet with government support. Even if you are financially comfortable, the issues of loneliness and illness remain, and possibly the pain of degenerative diseases such as dementia and arthritis. If a human's quality of life is so deeply compromised, can we claim that it's a blessing to have a lifespan of 100 or 200 years?

According to the World Population Prospects report released by the United Nations in July of 2022, global population growth fell below one percent in 2020 for the first time since 1950. The report predicted that the elderly population worldwide will increase from 10 percent in 2022 to

16 percent by 2050. In particular, concerns have been raised that China's aging population and decreasing productivity could lead to chronic "stagflation," with prices continuing to rise despite an economic recession worldwide. Some call the growing senior population the "silver tsunami," a trend that will be difficult to address with any short-term prescription. It means that the current system, which limits people's ability to contribute productively after a certain age, will reduce the quality of life for society in general.

The initial response we can make is to prepare at a personal level. Although it will take time for a system that supports an aging society to become mature, there are many things each individual can do before that. My 2017 book, *I've Decided to Live 120 Years,* offers a solution. This book contains my thoughts on how to reflect on the entire course of living and prepare for the second half of life to achieve a healthier, more rewarding, and more satisfying life experience overall.

In this book, I divided a 120-year life into two halves, with age 60 as the halfway point. If the first half of life is for growth and achievement, the second half is centered on sharing, giving back, and letting go. It's very much like breathing, which is a cycle of inhalation and exhalation. Observing and planning life with a long-term perspective can make our lives more rewarding, balanced, and fulfilling.

In addition, we must work together to prepare a societal system that enables meaningful and valuable social contributions and interactions throughout our lives. When society strives for coexistence, we will have many more opportunities to use the wisdom and empathy brought through the experiences of a long life.

Social contributions and interactions made during the later years are essential for more than just the economy. They improve people's quality of life by providing opportunities to actualize internal values, such as life gratification and character maturation, that no social service system can provide. At the same time, as witnessed in many traditional tribal communities, they can help a community by offering a balanced perspective and peaceful solutions to conflict. Providing the elderly with opportunities for social contribution and using those contributions as an asset of wisdom for the entire community is a measure of how mature and healthy that community is. It is each individual's responsibility to become a senior citizen who is benevolent and wise, but the community must create the space and opportunities for that love and wisdom to be shared.

Longevity as a Blessing to Everyone

In the 1930s, social security systems were implemented in many economically advanced countries, including the United States, primarily to provide financial support for the retired elderly population. At the time, the average life expectancy at birth in the US was 58 to 62 years. Based on a retirement age of 65, the remaining life of those who survived until then averaged about 13 to 15 years. In other words, when the social security system was created, no one expected people to live very long after retirement.

Back then, the life cycle was predictable: upbringing and education until about 20, economic activities from the 20s to the 60s, and retirement at 65 or so. Retirees then lived the rest of their lives on income from their savings and the social welfare system. At that time, the populations in each age range mainly interacted with others in the same range. These days, more and more people are living into their 90s and 100s. Yet, there aren't sufficient personal financial resources and societal systems to allow people to maintain their human dignity beyond the age of 65. People may not be able to engage in physical activities past 60 like they did in their youth, but they can help society with their emotional maturity and wisdom. Under the current systems, however, these qualities are not being utilized as societal assets but are simply going to waste.

We cannot resolve the issue of aging only in terms of welfare funding that merely supports survival because it is not just an economic matter. What's more important is to live a dignified and rewarding life. We need to develop personal life plans and social support systems fitting for an era when life expectancy is 100 years and a new fulfilling chapter of life *starts* at age 60.

Whether young or old, having the opportunity to meet, interact with, learn from, and contribute to members of different levels of society is hugely helpful for discovering the value of life. I have confirmed this by observing the changes in many students who attended the Benjamin School for Character Education. Students can interact with people of various ages, occupations, and social classes through volunteer work or mentoring while carrying out their chosen projects. For example, as the elderly tell young students about their own experiences and the students help them with tasks that are difficult for them to do alone, both sides can learn and grow through their connection with one another. Such experiences are hard to come by within a homogeneous group.

Above all, the earth's environment must recover enough healthy balance to sustain extended lives. And emotional inclusion and wisdom, which can be nurtured in the maturity of old age, need to be recognized as critical societal values. We can create a culture that supports transmitting these values to younger generations. Material conditions such as lifelong educational opportunities and welfare systems that support such a culture are also essential. A happy, long life should not result from individual luck or effort but from a society working together with a shared, caring spirit.

Suggestions for Healthy and Rewarding Later Years

Since institutional and systemic changes aren't achieved only through individual efforts, they take time. However, a shift in how old age is perceived can begin now. You can plan to fill the last half of your life with meaningful activities that contribute to society and humankind. Sharing ideas and thoughts and initiating conversations about this, which we can start right away, will inspire one another to co-create nationwide change eventually.

To begin, I'd encourage you to decide on a life expectancy for yourself. We can't control our lifespan in whatever way we decide, but there are many advantages to choosing our lifespan.

First, you can better manage your health if you aim to live to a certain age. No one would want to live to be 100 or 120 years old while suffering from illness and needing to be cared for by others. By choosing your life expectancy, you'll take a greater interest in how you live your day-to-day life and make a more active effort to develop a healthy lifestyle and attitude.

Next, you can have a long-term picture of your own life. Rather than retiring sometime between the age of 60 and 70 and then living as if the life you have after that is a bonus, you'll adopt a goal of growth and self-realization that you can pursue for the rest of your life. Instead of being a period of decline, this "second half" of your life can be your golden years. You can become more mature and complete a foundation of diverse social experiences from the first half of your life.

Finally, you can make better and wiser decisions. Looking at the results of your choices through a long frame of reference, you can consider long-lasting effects and consequences over immediate benefits. This process will lead to making choices that will be helpful both to yourself and to others.

For healthy and rewarding later years, I suggest the following practices that you can do as an individual.

Positive and Close Interpersonal Relationships

Harvard Medical School conducted an interesting study on adult development to find what factors most affect people's quality of life, health, and longevity over the long haul. This project, which began in 1938 with 268 participants and spanned 80 years, is famous for being the longest study in academic research history. What do you think were the conclusions?

It turns out that the most significant long-term factor affecting people's quality of life and longevity was neither financial competence nor social success. It was close, positive relationships. Many other studies have shown similar conclusions—including, for example, that loneliness threatens health as much as smoking or drinking does.

What is the quality of your relationships with other people? What efforts are you making to cultivate positive and intimate relationships? Here are some questions to help you evaluate your relationships:

- *Do you have someone to talk to when you are sad or worried at night?*
- *Is there someone who won't mind if you let yourself be at ease and act silly around them?*
- *Do you have someone with whom you can share your thoughts without worrying that they will think you're weird?*

You are fortunate if you can answer "yes" to even one of these questions. Many people cannot share their painful wounds with anyone, so they wrestle with their burdens alone. Many people can't relax, even in their most intimate relationships, because they want to look appealing or virtuous, strong, smart, or pretty to others. Countless people can't be open about their feelings because they're afraid of being judged by others.

If you have someone who makes it possible for you to say "yes" to the previous questions, thank them from the bottom of your heart. Pour more sincere devotion and effort into developing that relationship. The power, comfort, and joy you gain from such a relationship will protect your body and mind from disease and help you thrive in the era of centenarians.

Positive Thoughts and Emotions

An interesting experiment showed how significantly positive thinking and emotions affect the health of both mind and body, especially in old age. This experiment was part of the "Counterclockwise" study led by Harvard psychologist Dr. Ellen Langer in 1979.

Two groups of people in their 70s and 80s took part in the experiment. With eight people in each group, subjects participated in a week-long retreat where the environment was decorated as if it were 1959. The control group was asked to spend a week simply reminiscing about their lives in 1959. The experimental group was instructed to act as if it were actually 1959, speaking and behaving as if they were 20 years younger.

A week later, both the control group and the experimental group showed improvement. As their skeletal structure straightened, they became taller. Their joints became more flexible, and their fingers straightened and became longer as arthritis disappeared. Their eyesight and hearing also improved, as did their memory.

Most of those improvements were much more signifi-cant in the group told to live as if it were actually 1959. A full 63 percent of them had better intelligence test scores at the end of the experiment than they did at the beginning, compared to 44 percent in the control group. On the last day of the study, Langer wrote, men who had seemed so frail just days before ended up playing an impromptu touch football game on the front lawn. Their biological age itself had been "turned back."

Changes in mood and emotional state can be explained by neuroplasticity or hormonal changes. But it's impossible to explain physical transformation this way. This sort of improvement requires change at the genetic level, including the regeneration of cells. In that sense, this experiment showed how powerful an impact changes in thoughts, emotions, and behavior could have.

Thoughts and emotions are one type of habit. If any repeated pattern is unhealthy and doesn't help you or anyone else, it's best to change it. Just as we change unhealthy eating habits such as overeating or binge eating, we need to make an effort to recognize and change patterns of thought or emotions that aren't helpful to us.

There are many ways to change our thoughts and emotions. Exercise, body posture, facial expression, focused breathing, and meditation can be beneficial. Don't stay in it when you've slipped into a pattern of thoughts or emotions that you don't want. Don't even try to change it with your thoughts or feelings. Jump up and stretch, do push-ups or squats, or rub your hands to create heat and then sweep down your face and whole body. It's much easier to change your energy by moving your body than by trying to change your thoughts.

One way to change your energy that's simple and effective is to smile. Many experiments have confirmed that even a forced smile changes hormone secretion in the brain in a mere 20 to 30 seconds. Without arguing over why this happens, lift the corners of your mouth, relax your lips, and smile. Think of this as a meditation, and try to hold the smile for at least a minute or two. You'll find it hard to have negative thoughts or emotions in that state.

If you are under stress, with your head full of negative thoughts and emotions, I recommend taking three deep breaths before saying or doing anything. While taking those breaths, your energy will change and your thoughts and emotions will become different, helping you avoid saying or doing anything that you'll later regret.

Though thoughts and emotions might seem transient, negative thoughts and feelings leave traces. These traces build up and can lead to depression, memory loss, and even degenerative brain disease. When elderly people in rural areas living long and healthy lives were asked about the secret to longevity, they often laughed and said, "I didn't do anything special." What's special is the mindset of not having to do anything special to live a long life and the mind that sees everything in a positive way with joy and gratitude even for small things.

Sufficient Physical Activity

Everyone knows the effect of exercise on physical health. But did you know exercise also plays a major role in brain health? Exercise has been found to slow the aging of cells, preventing degenerative brain diseases and even helping to generate new brain cells. Many different types of exercises can achieve this. Aerobic exercise stimulates the brain and helps activate brain cells by increasing oxygen supply. Muscle exercise helps maintain memory and builds confidence and willpower. Relaxation exercises such as breathing and meditation help reduce stress responses and promote positive emotions.

In an interview with the *Los Angeles Times*, researcher Dr. James Levine of the Mayo Clinic, one of the top medical institutions in the United States, stated, "Sitting is more dangerous than smoking, kills more people than HIV, and is more treacherous than parachuting. We are sitting ourselves to death." According to Dr. Levine, most people in the US spend more than half their waking hours being sedentary.

Exercise doesn't mean you must go to the gym or use special equipment. What matters is that you get up and move your body. Walking for 30 minutes a day or doing squats or push-ups are all good exercises. The important thing is to move your body every chance you get. Try to move your body at least once an hour, even if it's just for a minute. That one minute will be more helpful than anything else you do for keeping your brain and body energetic and healthy for a life of 100 or even 120 years.

A Life Purpose

The question "Do you have a clear goal for your life?" might seem cliché. But having a life purpose is the most significant factor in life achievement, even more critical than personal abilities or environments. I've confirmed this through my own experience, and many studies have reached similar conclusions.

What is my goal in life? When did you first ask yourself this question? When was the last time you thought about it? What would your answer be if you asked yourself this question? The human brain changes until the moment we take our last breath. What remains at the conclusion of life are the understanding, insight, and feelings about life that we get as the total of our experiences. So as long as you feel anything in your heart and your brain remains active, it's never too late. A great awakening that can make the meaning of your life completely different can come at any moment. Therefore, regardless of how much you have accomplished, I recommend you pose this question to yourself again and choose a life goal.

Usually, when we're choosing a goal, we ask what we want most. Many people charge forward to achieve their goals without looking to the side or behind themselves. But even though they may achieve a goal that way, they have a sense of emptiness and may even get the feeling that they've wasted their life. If you want to avoid feeling something is missing, I recommend asking the following two questions before asking yourself what you most desire. Asking these questions will help you live a life you won't regret.

The first question I introduced in Chapter 3: *"How do I want to be remembered when my life comes to an end?"* This question helps discover fundamental desires from a place far deeper than the ego. No matter what kind of life we've led until now or what type of person we've deemed ourselves to be, most of us want to be remembered as someone who has contributed to the world. In a place deeper than selfish instinct, every human being has the instinct of Hongik—the desire to do something good for the world.

The second question to ask yourself is, *"How do I want to feel?"* Answering this question gives our choices and life paths a clearer and more intuitive sense of guidance than just having sensible thoughts. It's through that feeling that we ultimately verify the achievement of our lives. Let's say that you've achieved a specific goal. If you're not significantly different from most people, you don't accept that you've completed your purpose in life only through external achievements. Most people check this through what they feel in their hearts. If they don't feel anything and there's no sense of satisfaction, they'll probably think, *"This wasn't it,"* and they'll ask again, "What is it that I really want?" That's why the question of how you want to feel is essential to ask.

There will be a certain feeling you want, such as a sense of fulfillment, confidence, pride, dignity, and having no regrets. When you've confirmed that feeling, ask yourself what would make you feel that way. What you want might differ from what you *think* you want or *should* want. What makes you happy and gives you a sense of fulfillment in life may be closer than you expect.

The specific expression for the feeling you want can vary from person to person, but the closest word to encapsulate them all is probably "completion." Completion is neither overflowing nor insufficient, with neither regret nor things left undone. And there is gratitude for the opportunities in life that were given to us, love and blessings for everyone we got to meet in that life, and fearless expectation for the remaining journey. When you've reached the feeling of completion, the only thing remaining as the last image of your life may be the hint of a smile at the corners of your mouth. And that will say everything about your life.

Pursuing self-development and success and this kind of completion will enable you to live a more balanced and full life. And the experiences and insights you gain through such a life will contribute to helping even more people reach this goal of completion and advance a culture of coexistence throughout all of society.

Life as a Comprehensive Gift Set

One of the profoundly uncomfortable truths that we all acknowledge but don't want to accept is death. People like to avoid talking about it because it's painful, but nothing in our lives is as guaranteed as death. Frankly, death is the only certainty in a life full of change and uncertainty.

This reality is why our attitude toward death is so contra-dictory. Even though it is inevitable, we think and act as if it doesn't exist. Conversations about death are uncomfortable and avoided in most of our day-to-day activities. There's a perception that death isn't something to be addressed by ordinary folks, only by extraordinary people with religious authority. So, despite death being the most important life event anyone experiences, we receive neither guidance nor education about it. At a time when science and technology are as highly developed as they are now, thoughts about death remain within the domain of religious authority. It wouldn't be an exaggeration to say that they're staying at the level they were during medieval times.

Not one of us chose our environment when we were born. The circumstances of life we encounter after birth are given to us regardless of our likes and dislikes. But death is different. I can choose what kind of state I will die in, with what kind of mindset. Although this is not yet accepted in many cultures, I think that I should even be able to choose the time and manner in which I will die. In the future, I believe there will be many changes in our thoughts and attitudes toward natural lifespans and life itself.

Saying that life is a gift doesn't mean only the beginning of life. Life is a comprehensive gift set that includes the beginning and the end. If the start of life is a gift, so is the end. It's not something where the beginning is welcome and celebrated while the end is to be feared and avoided. No matter how hard life may be, there is an end where you can set down all of your burdens and be free. No matter how sweet and beautiful life may be, there is an end that makes you break free from flashy illusions and attachments and see things as they are. Despite the sadness of parting, death opens up opportunities for healing, awakening, and freedom for those who are leaving and those who remain. Thus death is not a disaster for life forms but a gift, a right, and an opportunity.

As a complete gift bundle, death makes life complete. This fact does not come about through physical conditions or any social welfare system but with the support of a spiritual awakening to a greater understanding of life. Such a spiritual awakening expands our consciousness so we can see life not only as the metabolic function of a physical body but as a large circulation of energy that encompasses all beings.

While alive, if we know the roots of our existence and accept this life in a physical body as part of the magnificent flow of life, we understand that our life is eternal, regardless of birth and death. Based on this awareness, if you've devoted your life to upholding truthfulness according to your inner light, love, conscience, and compassion, the death that you meet at its end will be an honor and a blessing.

CHAPTER 10

Technology Respecting the Value of Life

"It's not a faith in technology. It's faith in people."

— Steve Jobs

I am primarily analog, whether judged by my age or my tastes. Most of what I usually teach people—breathing, energy sensitivity, a cool head, a warm belly, and a comfortable chest—is based on analog sensibilities and approaches. When educating or doing business, I've thought it more important than anything else to meet and communicate with people directly.

When I suddenly couldn't meet anybody in person one day due to the pandemic, it was as if my hands and feet were tied. What can I communicate to people if we can't move our bodies in the same space, sharing energy and feeling each other's reactions? It was confusing and frustrating. As the pandemic dragged on, just like everyone else, I adopted online versions of workshops and retreats that had once been face-to-face programs. Although by then I was more used to virtual meetings than before the pandemic, it was the first time I'd ever done a workshop or retreat online. I assumed I shouldn't expect the same level of intimacy and solidarity that I had from face-to-face conversations.

The Art of Coexistence

Such concerns turned out to be groundless. It took some time, but we had no difficulty connecting and sharing experiences online. Even through a screen, I could feel the breathing and energy of the participants, and we could share each other's joy and pain. Their earnestness and passion in searching for soul-satisfying meaning and purpose in life reached me unaltered. Our encounter was even more effective and powerful than a face-to-face meeting because now countless people could connect and share the same experience, unconstrained by time and space.

In the end, what mattered was our attitude toward one another. Our method wasn't an issue as long as we could communicate heart to heart. Today's wonderful information and communications technologies and devices help make communication more effective, provided it carries our hearts. Conversely, such means of communication are no better than a passed note unless our minds are open and interconnected.

What indicates the current level of communication between people isn't how much data they use. Considering the amount of data involved, we should be able to communicate 10 times, even 100 times better than we did a decade ago—but we are not doing so. Our lives are still marked by disagreement, prejudice, exclusion, and bullying. We use "connectivity" as a collective term referring to technologies linking people with devices and devices with each other. But while technology can create conditions allowing people to link up, it doesn't connect them heart-to-heart.

Heart-level connection is essential not only in communication technology, but also in other promising technologies in order to change life effectively. The goal of many new technologies is to let us do more of what we already do, faster and more conveniently. But while new technologies may increase productivity and lower costs, on a larger scale, they also can cause us to create more waste. With technologies alone, we cannot solve our present predicament. What must change are our hearts, our choices, and our practices.

The Challenge of the Fourth Industrial Revolution

In March 2016, Google's AlphaGo computer program competed against Go game world champion Sedol Lee. Contrary to the expectations of numerous people, this "match of the century" ended in an overwhelming four-to-one victory for artificial intelligence (AI). This outcome shocked many and gave rise to worrying predictions about humankind. AI is broadly changing our daily lives as it is used in scientific research and almost all areas of life, including online shopping and social media.

With the advent of AI, the Fourth Industrial Revolution has become a topic of interest. Since the concept was first mentioned in 2016 at Davos in Switzerland, the forum where political, cultural, and business leaders from around the world exchange ideas and information on the direction of global change, the discussion of the Fourth Industrial Revolution has continued to expand. Because of the ripple effects new technologies will have on our lives, people everywhere—not only scientists and technologists—are keeping an eye on these changes.

The First Industrial Revolution was about mechanization based on the steam engine's invention. The Second Industrial Revolution brought mass production using new energy sources such as petroleum and electricity. The Third Industrial Revolution can be said to have involved the spread of information through computers. Now, the Fourth Industrial Revolution brings the functions of computers closer to those of humans and makes computers smart enough to replace human intellectual functions.

Examples of the Fourth Industrial Revolution include: the "Internet of Things" connecting almost all devices and tools as well as computers, a high-speed communication network enabling real-time exchange between these things, and quantum computer technology capable of processing in minutes calculations that would take supercomputers hundreds of years.

The first three industrial revolutions rapidly increased human productivity, letting us enjoy material abundance. But serious problems have arisen, including social inequality and environmental destruction, threatening the welfare and survival of our entire species. Rapidly unfolding at a time when such issues haven't yet been resolved, the Fourth Industrial Revolution poses challenges on a whole new level.

As we increasingly use humanoid robots equipped with AI, many concerns are being raised, including fears about safety and reduced employment opportunities. Elon Musk, CEO of Tesla, a front-runner in humanoid robot development, has said that robots will replace humans primarily in "simple, repetitive, tedious, and dangerous tasks." Now, though, AI does more than that, having moved on to poetry and painting. The paintings are even sold on the art market. Virtual human models seen in advertisements are almost indistinguishable from real people. If a robot body that looks like an actual human can perform far superior functions, how many jobs requiring humans will remain?

Many people already spend much more of their time with digital media than with other people. If humanoid robots are introduced into private life, how much of our lives will remain "human" in the future?

The above are examples of different ways technology affects our lives. What's common to most advanced technologies is that they, and the monopolistic capital behind them, wield enormous power and influence over people. Furthermore, the development of technology has changed the status of humanity. Many people have raised concerns about the negative impact the few can have with exclusive control over capital and technology. Yet their power is outpacing efforts to regulate it legally.

Control of information and technology has been concentrated in a few corporations and organizations, and access to information is unequal; this is already the reality experienced by everybody. Moreover, we lose or give up autonomy because of technology's control over our consciousness through customized information and our deepening reliance on algorithms and AI. From the loss of labor opportunities to a digital dictatorship ruling the individual psyche and behavior, the possibilities the Fourth Industrial Revolution could bring are genuinely concerning.

Of course, the future of technology is not written in stone; many less-gloomy possibilities lie before us. The

Fourth Industrial Revolution enables us to optimize production and consumption on a global scale. By doing this, we can create a society of abundance, allowing us all to maintain our dignity as human beings while minimizing our ecological footprint. All people can be liberated from laboring for survival to realize their value and contribute to society through their chosen activities. Everyone can enjoy life through a generously extended lifespan without worrying about disease and pain. In this way, the Fourth Industrial Revolution can provide the material conditions and technological means to realize our potential for a utopian life once possible only in our imaginations.

The Fourth Industrial Revolution provides an unprecedented opportunity to overcome social inequality and environmental degradation to create a harmonious, healthy, prosperous global community. But at the same time, in direct contrast, it could make our continued survival as a species on this planet impossible. There has never been a generation carrying such potential and risk in human history and bearing responsibility for a choice of such magnitude.

We call ourselves *Homo sapiens*, the wise humans, but we cannot say whether wisdom characterizes our species more than anything else. Human intelligence is outstanding, but whether it is a curse or a blessing remains an open question. Our intellect cannot be called wisdom if it causes us to pursue only our immediate interests, ultimately leading to our destruction.

We need thoughtful wisdom, not mere intelligence, to guide us on saving ourselves and other living things. Such brilliant wisdom cannot be found in microscopes, telescopes, or supercomputers or on the Internet. It is located within ourselves, in our minds and hearts.

Simultaneously open before us are contradictory possibilities like these. Which of them is realized depends on our awareness and our choices. This challenge is posed to us by the Fourth Industrial Revolution.

True Human Value

Recovering our humanity is the key to wisely navigating the challenges of the Fourth Industrial Revolution. This recovery means finding our existential value as individuals and as a species.

Humans have acquired evolutionary superiority over other animals and reached the top of the pecking order in Earth's current ecosystem because of their intellectual capabilities. Assessments of "competent" in almost all cultures involve intellectual ability. And for many, being "smart" is a matter of pride. Now, with the development of AI, the human whose self-image is centered on intellectual capabilities faces a fundamental challenge. What took a hit in the match with AlphaGo was not the pride of a single Go player but humanity's self-image as the pinnacle of creation.

A definite advantage of AI over humans is that it can exclude prejudice and emotion from its choices and determinations. In theory, AI can make optimal decisions regarding all the problems we face, provided that the quantity and quality of its data are guaranteed.

Imagine that we took the most advanced AI and asked it this question: "What is the fastest and most effective way to restore the planet's ecosystem?" What response would it produce? An answer probably comes to mind, though we might not want to say it out loud. Unless our consciousness and way of life change, why should we continue to exist on Earth while causing suffering for our fellow humans and countless other organisms? What is the actual value of humanity?

If intellectual ability is no longer unique to humans—as the technological achievements of AI have shown—what is the quality that makes humans truly human? As I stressed early in this book, characteristics unique to humans as beings who have self-awareness are *empathy*, *conscience*, and *introspection*.

It is because we have a conscience that we can choose the truth even at the risk of personal disadvantage, and we can prioritize the good of all when the interests of the whole conflict with our own. Because we have the capacity for introspection, we gain insight through experience by looking back on ourselves. Furthermore, we are curious about our origins, asking, "Who or what am I?" Along with these two traits, what makes humans human—and what is needed for a sustainable planet—is empathy. Because we have empathy, humans can feel other people, other life, and other objects as if they are ourselves, and we can voluntarily act in ways that help others.

In a social system centered on competition and domination, intellectual ability has always been prioritized. Empathy was treated as a secondary value, or even suppressed because it didn't help beat the competition. We are now staring nakedly into the abyss, seeing how intellectual ability without concern for other people, other groups, and other life forms can devastate the foundation of our lives.

Humanity's true value and greatness can come to light when intellectual ability and empathy are integrated. Intelligence has more value when it is used to express empathy, not to suppress it. Humans alone have the conditions and capabilities to do that. This is why, though the species has not yet fully shown this aspect of itself, humanity remains the hope of Earth. Humanity is the hope of all life on the planet. I firmly believe that we have the power to make that hope a reality.

Convergence of Humanity and Technology

AI becoming more powerful than all human intelligence combined is commonly called the "singularity." Given the exponential and accelerating pace of AI development, many experts predict that the singularity will arrive within the generation of humans now living on Earth.

What position is there for humanity when machine intellect exceeds the sum of all human intelligence? To answer this question, we must ask what the nature of humanity is. The history of Earth stretches back 4.5 billion years, but it has only been 4 million years since the human species, in the broadest sense, first appeared. Modern humans, *Homo sapiens*, came on the scene no more than 200,000 to 300,000 years ago. If the time from the planet's birth to the present were a 24-hour day, then the span of modern human existence would be no more than 3.8 seconds. Overly focused on ourselves, we lose sight of the magnificent evolution of life that has been going on throughout Earth's entire history. For us, human life is precious and prominent. Yet it is a short scene in the long play of biological evolution.

Before modern humans, survival and reproduction were the natural world's most significant drivers of evolution. Animals have evolved in directions advantageous for finding food and mates and spreading their genes. But these biological drivers of evolution have virtually disappeared from modern civilization. We no longer need to run faster or have stronger muscles to find food or mates.

What if a path allowing continuous evolution were open to humanity, a species that has virtually lost the need and potential for biological evolution? What would that path be? I think it might be a spiritual awakening and expansion of consciousness on the one hand and a fusion of humans and machines on the other. We are already experiencing a convergence of humans and machines in our daily lives. Through our mobile devices, we connect with many others and communicate unrestricted by time or space, grasping what is happening around the world in real time. The information, range of consciousness, and interests we now have probably put us well beyond most sages or enlightened masters of the past. Technological progress has incredibly impacted our consciousness without us even realizing it.

Humans and technology are intimately connected physically, too. How much of the day do we spend without accessing the Internet? How much time do we spend with a mobile phone in hand? Cell phones already function like a part of our bodies. We hold our phones in our hands now, but before long, we might accept the idea of installing the functions we need directly into our bodies, as we already do for artificial organs and equipment such as pacemakers.

Once the scope of human activity moves beyond the Earth in the not-too-distant future, our bodies will probably be too weak and brittle to support our species' exploration and pioneering activities. Our bodies can't withstand gravitational forces several times that of our home planet. They are unlikely to last even a century on Earth, though we feed them, wash them, and care for them daily.

The current human is a being trapped in a physical body and ruled by emotions rooted in that body. But the body doesn't ultimately need to be the limit of humanity. The vessel holding human consciousness and information doesn't necessarily have to be a body like the one we have now. Artificial organs are already in use; in the future, more body parts may be replaced by artificial constructs. Later, in the definition of "human," the boundary between biological and engineered elements may break down. The material form itself might become meaningless. What is the essence of humanity, and what is the essence of life? These are the crucial questions. What remains, in the end, is consciousness—and the information contained in that consciousness.

The confrontation between humans and machines is a staple of Hollywood movies. In many novels depicting a dystopian Earth, this is portrayed as a significant social conflict of the future. But the line between humans and

The Art of Coexistence

machines is already blurred, and convergence is already happening. Amid such change, it would be meaningless to talk of a confrontation between humans and machines. Machines and humans, artificial intelligence and natural intelligence—the relationship between them doesn't need to be antagonistic, and convergence in one form or another is likely.

The real problem is not a confrontation between biologically defined humans and machines but a conflict between consciousness and consciousness, information and information. It's about what kind of consciousness and what kind of information moves the organism in which man and machine are fused. Is this happening for coexistence or domination and destruction? These choices will determine the future of Earth and humanity. Choosing the goal of coexistence can give meaning and direction to the Fourth Industrial Revolution.

The Fifth Industrial Revolution

The Fourth Industrial Revolution that's currently taking place has amazing potential. We can find answers to complex problems—issues we've been unable to resolve because of their scale, such as climate change and ecosystem restoration—and even develop the technological means to implement them. We can realize a government freeing us from worries over moral corruption and degradation through objective, fair, and transparent administrative services. We can eliminate poverty and inequality by improving productive capacity and optimizing distribution. We can provide many people with safe jobs and more leisure by letting machines handle the hard, hazardous work.

Of course, the opposite is also a definite possibility. A small number of individuals and groups monopolizing capital and technology may rule the world as they wish. Many may live passive lives day after day, without goals, hopeless and helpless—isolated individuals who've lost control of their own lives. For now, that picture looks more realistic. This situation is why, along with technological advancement, we urgently need a change in consciousness and behavior that will give purpose and direction to the Fourth Industrial Revolution. I believe that change must become the Fifth Industrial Revolution.

The Fifth Industrial Revolution will lead the Fourth, providing it with goals and direction. In that sense, the Fifth Industrial Revolution is not a movement of the future arising *after* the Fourth Industrial Revolution but one happening *alongside* it. But suppose the Fourth Industrial Revolution, directed solely toward technological development, continues without such changes. In that case, it may signal the start of a suicidal implosion of human civilization instead of a revolution leading to a better future. The Fifth Industrial Revolution is not a technological disruption but a living culture *innovating* industry through an awakening of consciousness.

Therefore, this is a revolution in which everyone—not just scientists and engineers—can and should participate. Through the Fifth Industrial Revolution, by using the technological achievements of the Fourth Industrial

Revolution for coexistence, we can create a peaceful, healthy, sustainable world for all living things, not just the human species. Such changes will let us achieve a genuinely global community and move forward into a greater space age as a responsible, mature civilization.

CHAPTER 11

True Welfare, the Social Foundation of Coexistence

"There are two principles of justice: not to harm anybody and to serve society's welfare."

— Cicero

How would you answer if someone asked, "Are you happy now?" People's answers don't appear to change in proportion to rising living standards. Positive changes in the average level of education, culture, medical care, and income don't increase individual happiness once basic needs are met. The opposite is more often the case. A big reason for personal unhappiness is a *relative* sense of poverty and deprivation.

Commonly expressed in South Korea as being born with either a golden or a dirt spoon in one's mouth, economic inequality is a problem in virtually all the world's nations, regardless of their level of economic development. Every major shock to the financial system—such as the bursting of the dot-com and real estate bubbles or the recent COVID pandemic—has widened the gap between the rich and poor and deepened inequality.

The expression "10 to 90" is often used when discussing economic inequality. It means that the wealth of 10 percent of the world's population equals the combined wealth of the remaining 90 percent. As this gap is deepening, many people are even using the phrase "1 to 99." Many in the 90 percent feel frustrated as their chances of moving toward the 10 percent by personal effort are dwindling.

Along with the perceived difference in wealth, the unfairness of inequality makes things harder for people. Through historical experience, we have seen that unfair inequality, not inequality itself, brings social division and, if neglected, leads to the collapse of society. Fair rules lie at the heart of a just society, and fair equality must be established based on those rules.

True welfare is realized when community care is added to this foundation of institutional fairness. When we think of welfare, we often think of economic policies or medical systems that support the underprivileged. But welfare assists and can be applied to everyone, not just the socially vulnerable. Public care helps all community members maintain human dignity and realize their values. In that sense, welfare is not just an institution but a culture and a spirit. Welfare is the basic foundation for achieving coexistence at the social level.

Fairness and Equality

No country in the world completely entrusts its economy solely to the logic of the market. If left to the market to decide, excessive inequality and relative poverty would quickly become a major source of social unrest. The laws and systems currently applied in most capitalist market economies have been revised and supplemented with programs like free education and retirement programs to address the imbalances of free market capitalism over time.

Nations that have pursued equality as an ideal goal have experienced greater changes than capitalist countries over the past half-century. Forced and indiscriminate equality reached its limit. Such equality was ruthless, unfair, uninteresting, and unable to provide an impetus for creation and change. Beginning with the collapse of the Soviet Union at the end of the twentieth century, forced equality is being gradually abandoned as a social system. Few countries now maintain principled socialism, and even in countries claiming to be socialist, the gap between the rich and the poor grows daily.

In any system, fairness is ultimately the key. Equality must be fair, not indiscriminate. Having equality based on fairness can be surprisingly simple: like runners in a race, we all start at the same line and are recognized and rewarded according to the results. This concept of fairness and equality is understandable to anyone.

The first question regarding fairness is whether everyone starts from the same line. When some are born without advantages, and others can claim, "part of my skill is being born well-off," frustration and conflict arise in society. Although generations could live off their wealth, others have lofty intentions, saying they'll leave their children only enough for them to lead healthy, respectable lives. Cases like this offer praiseworthy models for society, but hopes that our social system will be improved merely by personal awareness and goodwill are groundless.

No matter how high a cloud rises, it must return to the ground as rain if it is to rise again. Regardless of the tree's height, its seed must begin in the dirt. This process provides nature with stability while making diversity possible.

There are strict hierarchical orders among animals living in social groups, such as wolves, lions, and gorillas, and apparent inequalities in priorities for food and mates. However, new hierarchies are recreated constantly by new competitors; there is no known case in the animal kingdom of such hierarchical status being inherited by offspring. Nature does an excellent job of maintaining fairness and equality by beginning at the same starting line and ending in rewards based on results.

A second question to consider is whether so-called meritocracy—a system that begins at the same starting line and ends in different rewards based on results—is actually fair. Meritocracy has long been thought to offer rules for a fair game, an alternative to a caste system. Believers in meritocracy consider it only natural that they enjoy reasonable compensation for their achievements.

However, one example of social and economic inequality pointed out in many countries around the world is that prominent corporations' executives receive compensation hundreds or thousands of times that of ordinary employees through stock options. Shouldn't there be limits to rewards based on achievement levels? If we limit compensation levels, how much can we say is appropriate? How many of our achievements are due to our personal efforts and personal qualities? Is it safe to ignore the luck and chance that impact all of us just because we can't control them? What should we do about people who have the same skills but never get a chance to do anything with them?

Just because meritocracy and its resulting inequality are accepted now doesn't mean it's how things should be. Raising questions about this doesn't make you a socialist or a communist. This kind of labeling is neither productive nor beneficial nor applicable in today's diversified society. I suggest that instead of confining ourselves to the framework of left or right, progressive or conservative, we should open ourselves to all possibilities and look for a good system for everyone.

Even if a system equalizes the starting line and evaluates and compensates for results fairly, various gaps will still exist. Most people who lack ability or have no choice but to rely on the aid of others accept unequal living conditions without complaint. No matter how fair we make the game's rules, it won't be enough to solve this problem. Such gaps in society grow into wounds that putrefy; they are where collapse begins. Welfare isn't about squashing these gaps with ruthless equality rules but about filling them, bandaging them, preventing them from becoming diseased, and helping new flesh grow.

Welfare is not simply a matter of policies, rules, or institutions. Along with these things, it includes all the ways people relate to and care for one another. Welfare comprises all the elements of a mature community: respect for all humans and living beings; admiration and praise for the winners, along with humility and gratitude expressed by them; inspiration for all; and community care for those in need.

A Country of Happy People

The world is searching for a new welfare model. Northern European countries, once considered symbols of positive welfare systems, have also faced challenges, including increasing welfare costs, a discouragingly high tax rate for corporations and workers, and a negative impact on the motivation to work hard and innovate. Greece, which had implemented unconventional welfare policies under the motto, "Give the people everything they want," went into national bankruptcy in 2015 because it could not cope with the increased fiscal burden. Excessive benefits often create welfare dependency, making policies challenging to sustain.

Shrinking the welfare system intensifies social inequality and conflict while expanding it increases dependency on the state, putting pressure on national finances and reducing overall productivity and competitiveness. Consequently, we need a new approach, getting away from benefit systems centered on charity-like guarantees of material stability. A welfare system providing a safety net that includes basic food, clothing, and shelter is necessary, but what really matters is the quality of life and happiness experienced by people. A country where people are happy is a true welfare state.

By different indicators—such as life expectancy, medical care, income, and education—South Korea is far above average among member nations of the Organisation for Economic Co-operation and Development. However, as is well known, it ranks first worldwide for suicide. People are not happy. Instead of responding with suicide prevention programs, we need to think deeply and reflect on what makes us happy.

Material abundance alone doesn't create a country where people are happy. Psychologist Abraham Maslow's well-known hierarchy of needs provides crucial insights into well-being. Maslow established five levels of human needs, beginning with physiological needs and gradually developing into higher-level needs for safety, love and belonging, esteem, and self-actualization. Our sense of physical security has improved considerably with the introduction of basic welfare programs and may improve more in the future. However, benefit-based welfare programs do not satisfy social, esteem, and self-actualization needs. In fact, sometimes they do the opposite. No matter how much we increase welfare-related budgets and staffing, it won't solve the problem.

True welfare means understanding human needs at various levels and enabling all people to feel rewarded and happy by realizing their potential and maximizing their contribution to society and the world. An essential condition of such welfare is creating a culture in which all community members recover the goodness of humanity, developing a sense of coexistence, and in which coexistence is valued by that culture above all else.

No matter how excellent a welfare system may be, it will produce side effects such as laziness, inefficiency, unfairness, anger, and resentment unless supported by human conscience and a value system focused on coexistence. These traits must exist both among the people running the society and the citizens they serve. The foundation of true welfare isn't simply rules and systems but the hearts and minds of everyone. It is a mature community that considers the heart and mind valuable assets of society, nurturing and valuing them as much as any material resource.

Three Suggestions for Realizing True Welfare

I believe three things are necessary as the foundation of a welfare system for making a country's citizens happy. First are educational opportunities people can use to develop and grow throughout life. Second are opportunities to participate in and contribute to society, enabling people to feel rewarded and proud by playing positive roles in social relationships. And third is an income base allowing for the standard of living necessary to maintain a minimum level of self-esteem.

Historically, these three elements have been attempted in various ways by different cultures and countries. The Provisional Government of the Republic of Korea, when the country was struggling for independence from Japan, proposed them in its Three Principles of Equality, which it declared a founding philosophy. Although this did not become the permanent government of South Korea, the Three Principles of Equality did serve as an innovative, big-picture framework for the nation, combining the determination and hope to end Korea's colonial status with a passion for creating a system free of the conventions of the past. At the time, the Three Principles were, in the narrow sense, about creating an ideal society by bringing equality to politics, the economy, and education, and in the broader sense, about realizing a peaceful world by bringing equality to relations between peoples and nations.

This project may have been considered too idealistic at the time it was proposed; however, almost 80 years later, we now have the material and technological conditions for creating such a system. Some countries have already partially implemented these elements in their welfare systems. Though we still face many shortcomings, we can address these by adjusting the priorities of national goals, including the expected development of technology. I want to suggest in a little more detail the necessary conditions and roles for all of us in developing a country with a happy citizenry.

1. Equal Opportunities for Lifelong Education

The first condition for realizing welfare for all is a lifelong opportunity for education and economic support. Educational opportunities should always be open to everyone and expenses should be covered, provided you're sincere whenever you are ready and willing to learn.

Anyone who has been to school or has had the experience of educating children will know that there's no drudgery like studying without any motivation. However, many people are pushed into college with neither the desire nor any goal for studying. On the other hand, many cannot continue their studies because of external conditions, despite having reasons and a passion for learning. In other words, we can say that in the name of education, society is wasting a lot of time, effort, and resources and is creating a lot of stress.

Learning the principles necessary to be a sensible member of society doesn't take much time. We can learn in elementary school, or even in kindergarten, the essential basic principles we need in life. Even if it's reasonable to have compulsory education for a certain period, there's no need to tie almost all teenagers to preparing for college, as we do now in many competitive countries.

If we take all the time, effort, and resources wasted on needless courses and use them for people who *want* to study, that would leave more than enough to provide lifelong opportunities for education. It would be better to guide people who aren't motivated to study toward other opportunities to develop themselves and contribute to society instead of locking them in uniform educational institutions. Society's resources and institutions can help them once they develop a purpose and a reason to study.

Education is an individual effort to develop oneself, but it's also an investment by society in increasing quality of life and promoting continuous social development. Education offers a good return on investment, even purely economically. This reason should be enough to justify covering all educational expenses, at least for those with a purpose and the motivation to learn, provided they are sincere. For students who don't show sincerity, support could end, and they could continue their education at their own expense if they so desire. Many nations, including northern European countries with advanced welfare systems, provide education free of charge through college. This arrangement is not—and doesn't need to be—based on compassion or goodwill but on the rational calculation that educational outlays are investments that benefit society as a whole.

Educational opportunities do not need to be uniformly tailored by age. The motivation for education and the discovery of goals can develop at any time. It is also desirable for a nation when community members, regardless of age, have the opportunity to broaden their knowledge and improve their skills.

Mixing people of different ages and social experiences in the same educational program enriches the curriculum. It lets us share diverse wisdom and experiences not covered in the formal curriculum. It also creates opportunities to form the social networks we will need later. This arrangement has the advantage of leaving open lifelong opportunities for social interaction and contribution, which largely close after retirement for most people. This opportunity would contribute to a healthy old age and greatly help to create a more vital and balanced welfare system.

2. Equal Opportunities for Community Decision-Making

The second condition for creating a welfare system that benefits everyone is providing all citizens who meet age and other basic requirements with equal, diverse opportunities to participate in making large and small decisions for their local community and on a national level.

Democracy is based on the belief that power rests with the people. In reality, though, that belief is expressed in a country's constitution but most individual citizens don't feel that they are exercising any power. They may get that feeling only in the elections held once every few years.

The essence of power is decision-making. Of course, in democratic countries, individual citizens can exercise power in elections. But even that power merely lets them designate someone to make decisions on their behalf rather than take part directly. When the elections are over, the elected likely have no intention of involving voters in the decision-making process, and voters don't consider direct involvement their right or role.

Minimal representation is taken for granted in almost every country in the world. This system causes a sense of political helplessness and alienation and, among some, discontent and anger. "What do we know at the grass-roots level?" "It's the same no matter who gets elected." "Politicians are all thieving pieces of sh*t." Why do such self-deprecating sentiments arise? It's not because people are ignorant, incompetent, or disinterested in politics. It's not that they are malcontents struggling with life. They have motivation, an interest in society, and aspirations for a better world, but such sentiments take distorted forms when opportunities to express them are so limited.

Originally, democracy was not thought of as a representative system. In its purest form, democracy is exercising power with the people participating in the decision-making process. Examples of community members directly participating in decision-making are historically numerous, and this is still practiced in many communities.

The most significant reason why democracy became transformed into a representative system was procedural complexity. As a community grows, space and time constraints make it virtually impossible for all its members to be physically involved in decision-making. Additionally, as societies grow and diversify, they develop increasingly specialized domains. Ordinary citizens are unlikely to have enough expert knowledge to make proper judgments in all fields.

However, technological advances offer clues to solving these problems. The temporal and spatial constraints necessary for people to gather have almost entirely disappeared with the development of communication technologies and networks. Through the pandemic, we've grown accustomed to communications and decision-making that don't happen face-to-face. Online voting through social media to shape public opinion has become commonplace. Celebrities with many followers raise social issues individually and confirm public opinions through polls.

The reliability of security technologies has been the greatest obstacle to using online voting for elections. Many people doubt whether it's possible to tally online voting results accurately without manipulation or data errors. The most promising alternative is blockchain technology. This technology is for encrypting, distributing, and storing transaction records on each participant's computer instead of storing and managing them in one place. Being a decentralized system, no one can monopolize or control information, so it's advantageous for implementing direct democracy, in which everyone participates in decision-making.

As seen in the recent explosion of NFTs (non-fungible tokens or digital identifiers), blockchain technology also solved the problem of distinguishing between originals and replicas for digital art. With trust in its security growing, original digital art has become a significant investment target. If digital art can be secure enough to be an investment, then there is no reason the same technology cannot be applied to voting. It provides a powerful means for community members to participate in various forms of community decision-making without space or time limitations.

We can also solve the problem of expertise from a different angle. The most challenging part of the decision-making process for public administration is coming up with reasonable conclusions through rational analysis. Many interests are involved in this process, and there is certainly room for error. If administrators are troubled, it's because they cannot find the most reasonable conclusions or alternatives, not because they cannot make value judgments. Anyone with common sense and conscience can choose one of several practical and feasible options. But prejudice and selfish motives can intervene when choices are entrusted exclusively to a few because of their expertise. When it comes to rational analysis and reasoning, however, in a few years, no one will be able to surpass the abilities of AI.

In fact, AI already has these abilities. It's simply that AI utilization has been limited to fields such as social media and research and hasn't yet been applied to the public administration sector. Once AI is introduced in public administration, AI could replace most processes except for final selection and approval. Then processing will be much faster and more accurate, with less risk of error. If conclusions are reached through such a process or options are presented with clear pros and cons, anyone with common sense and conscience can judge what they think is best. Moreover, the risk of prejudice and selfish motives can be minimized if not one but several people participate in the final approval of an issue.

An interesting experiment was recently conducted regarding this, with results published in the international online journal *Nature Human Behaviour*. In this experiment, Google's AI developer DeepMind showed that AI can provide an equitable and rational method of virtual wealth distribution in an online investment game. After getting used to the game, participants played 20 rounds in which they decided how much of the money allocated to them at the beginning of the round they would contribute to a public investment fund. At the end of each round, money from the fund was distributed to all the participants based on different strategies. For a set of 10 rounds, a human strategy or a preset strategy determined the fund distribution. For the other 10 rounds, unknown to the participants, an AI program determined the strategy.

After the game, the researchers asked the participants which distribution strategy they preferred. The majority of the more than 4,700 participants preferred the AI-designed distribution criteria over almost all the others. It was also noted that the AI strategy appeared more neutral and responsive to the participants' actions than the human strategies. Although this was an experimental situation, it shows how AI can be used in collective decision-making processes to find solutions popular with the majority.

It won't be easy for everyone to be involved all the time, even in simple AI-assisted decision-making. We might envision an alternative system with community members participating in public administration on a rotational basis for set periods, especially for major decisions involving local to central governments. Many centuries ago, citizens of Athens and Sparta practiced such techniques, and modern jury systems today use the same approach.

If we can trust a randomly selected individual to have the common sense and conscience to pass a legal verdict, as in the present jury system, we have no reason not to do so on matters that are much less complex. Moreover, AI is expected to provide sufficiently reliable assistance in the process. AI is far more neutral, free of private interests, and indifferent to its reputation than the lawyers and prosecutors helping jurors make decisions in a lawsuit.

Directly participating in decision-making like this is an experience of actual power. Involvement in the decision-making process has had a very positive effect in countries where such policies are being implemented on a limited basis. When formulating welfare policies, many countries benchmark them against the social security systems of the so-called advanced welfare states of northwestern Europe. But one thing that's easy to miss is that direct democracy—including broad participation in public administration—is a significant strength of the institutions and cultures of those countries.

When this kind of participation is institutionalized, it has many positive impacts, including a sense of ownership in national management, monitoring fiscal soundness, and the morality of public officials. This arrangement significantly contributes to the health of welfare institutions in these countries. Participating in managing the community and country they belong to gives people an irreplaceable sense of pride, ownership, and responsibility.

Such attempts are necessary to prevent the dark shadow of a Big Brother society, which monopolizes information to monitor and dominate individuals. Inevitably, AI will be used more and more to support decision-making in the public and private sectors. Rather than fearing and avoiding such technology, we have to use it actively to build systems in which more people participate in decision-making. This system will help humanize technology and ensure that technology develops in harmony with community values.

3. Equal Basic Income Given at Birth

The third condition for creating a happy community is granting as a fundamental right of all citizens a source of basic income that can continuously generate revenue.

Gangs, drug dealing, and prostitution—problems in countries worldwide—are mainly lifestyle crimes. When growing up in an environment where you struggle to make ends meet and are exposed to crime, a person may accept this as a way of life. Of course, anyone can certainly choose a different path despite this. Not having the opportunity to experience a healthy way of life because of the environment one grew up in doesn't exempt anyone from responsibility.

But who would choose a life of lawlessness and crime if the opportunity to live a safe, healthy life in a safe, healthy environment were open to them? If people live in a healthy, civilized society, no one should have to choose suicide or crime, at least not because they lack life's basic necessities. If many people make such bad choices, community members should ask themselves whether the community is functioning as it should.

There's an old saying, "Not even the state can relieve poverty." Benefit-based welfare is not the way to fundamentally solve the problem. Giving may provide temporary help, but it fails to change the lives of beneficiaries radically and, consequently, to improve the well-being of the whole society. All welfare states have experienced the limits of benefit-based programs and struggle to find alternatives. If the goal is to overcome these limitations, a welfare program must provide recipients with the means to generate income rather than continuously giving unilateral, temporary help. In addition, it should help individuals proactively and responsibly manage those means. Such a program must be a right everyone enjoys as a community member, not help given only to the underprivileged.

Such an ideal system may seem like a fantasy, but attempts have been made to create such systems. Most were made at revolutionary turning points involving new dynasties or political systems, but almost all became twisted or wrecked. The most significant attempt to realize such ideas was undoubtedly communism, but as you know, that was a failed experiment. So the idea that we provide all citizens with an equal means of income still has a big question mark after it and is likely to raise many eyebrows. But if we change our thinking just a little, we can find ways to implement a high-level welfare program rationally.

In modern society, you don't have to run a factory or a farm to have a means of income. Through the convenient process of publicly traded shares, anyone can become the owner of a source of income to the extent they can afford. Numerous tools for individual investors allow anyone to start investing with a small amount if they wish.

Utilizing a system available to anyone, we could consider a program for creating an investment account in which a certain amount is deposited for each individual at the time of birth, using part of the welfare budget allotted for each citizen over a lifetime. The state would manage this account like a national pension until the owner reached a certain age when management rights would be transferred to the individual.

The idea of the government managing investment resources as a welfare fund benefiting all citizens is not new—think of Social Security in the United States and the National Pension Service in South Korea. What would be new is that participation in the program would be recognized as a fundamental right you have from birth, not something that begins when you get a job and start earning money. It would be a good idea to make sure economic education is mandatory for owners before they take over managing the accounts so that these accounts can function as a welfare guarantee for life. We could also make maintaining a minimum balance obligatory.

In countries with relatively stable capital markets, such as the United States, the return on stock investments averages more than 10 percent per year. In the United States, although the range of annual fluctuation is large, the average return since the 1950s, when official records began, has been 11.82 percent. Even if you estimate the rate of return more conservatively at 8 to 9 percent, the amount a newborn will have upon coming of age will be five times the initial deposit. For example, let's say you create an investment account for a newborn baby with $20,000 deposited at birth. Assuming an average annual return of 8 percent, if all proceeds are reinvested for 20 years, that will create an amount close to $100,000. If you have $100,000 in funds when you begin your life as an adult, you'll be off to a comfortable start.

Implementing such a system for the entire population would be financially impossible. However, it *could* be done for newborns. Taking South Korea as an example, the number of newborns was slightly over 260,000 in 2021. If 20 million KRW (approximately $16,000) is paid to everybody, the total amount is about 5.2 trillion KRW (more than $4 billion). As of 2021, the entire budget of the Korean government was 600 trillion KRW, with the welfare budget a little over 200 trillion KRW. Using 2.6 percent of the annual welfare budget and 0.85 percent of the total budget could create a basic source of income for all newborns—new members of the country. Having an economic foundation to start their lives independently when they come of age would greatly improve their quality of life.

Providing this support at the outset would significantly reduce the total cost of welfare benefits paid to individuals throughout their lives. This system could encourage childbirth by relieving the anxiety of young couples about their children's future. Although the amount of support might vary depending on the size or economic level of the population involved, these concepts and principles would be applicable in many countries seeking to realize more participatory and sustainable welfare systems.

Basic economics education is essential for such systems to have a significant impact. Rather than economic theory, we need to teach what money is and how to accumulate sound wealth. Such education would include that a life spent dependent on money from others is neither dignified nor stable and that learning how to fish is more helpful than being given fish. In this process, people also learn that it is difficult to accumulate wealth simply by not spending money and that compound interest is the greatest force moving behind money. Such a program would teach the principle of investing—letting money work for itself is the most effective way to accumulate wealth.

If you listen to stories of people who've achieved wealth, you'll hear that a reliable person often taught them basic money-related principles when they were young. They were also guided to practice these principles, turning them into habits. It would be difficult to expect all parents to give their children a basic education in managing money responsibly since parents often fail to set an example themselves. That's why such education needs to be provided by the state or country.

If we take it one step further, we could think of methods for equally distributing fiscal results to all citizens, like employee shareholders, applying to government finances a concept like that of a joint stock company. Taxes are collected differentially, but dividends are distributed evenly according to shareholder rights, which would have a substantial income-redistribution effect. Also, rather than looking for ways to save or evade taxes, people would monitor whether taxes are being collected correctly and whether the money is being used properly. Citizens would become the thrifty housekeepers of the nation.

It may sound impractical, but equal, direct payments from the state to its citizens have already been practiced in many countries, especially during the pandemic. Many measures have been taken to stimulate the economy during this challenging time. Among them, fiscal and financial policies such as tax rate and interest rate cuts affected capital markets, including stock markets, but had almost no effect on stimulating the real economy.

The most effective way to boost Main Street economy, an approach people can feel, is for governments to pay money directly and equally to every citizen who meets certain conditions. In the United States, "stimulus checks" signed by the president were sent to the public three times during the COVID pandemic. Introducing the concept of public shareholders for government finances and equally distributing fiscal surplus is similar to economic stimulus in distribution; the only difference is that the former would be carried out regularly, and that the funds would come from budgeted government tax revenue instead of newly printed cash, which will reduce the impact on potential inflation.

A system of national shareholders has several advantages. First, there is little possibility of distortion or irregularities since the process is simple and transparent. Unlike other welfare policies, it makes beneficiaries active participants rather than passive dependents—not receiving favors but confidently exercising one's rights. And as mentioned above, it creates a potent income-redistribution effect by distributing differentially collected taxes equally.

To test the process, it could be a good idea for a local government with sound finances to operate a pilot program. Implementation would vary depending on the circumstances, but at the heart of this approach is making citizens true owners of their country.

The Three Principles of Equality—equally distributing educational opportunities, the exercise of power, and the means of earning income—provide a solid foundation for a welfare system. Neither the system nor new technologies, including AI, allow these institutions to take root, blossom, and bear fruit. The subjects of welfare are not the state, corporations, or the rich, but human beings.

Welfare isn't something to be created by some individual and provided to the socially vulnerable; it's made by all members of society together. Based on the Three Principles of Equality, each individual must choose to live as a contributor rather than a beneficiary of welfare. As long as we can afford it even a little, we should be willing to help others and the world, being aware that doing so is our responsibility and a source of pride as community members. Conscience and empathy are what enable us to have this attitude. Fortunately, these two things are already in the hearts and minds of all people.

Ultimately, the purpose of welfare is to help realize the beautiful, noble nature of humanity. Even Confucius said that we know courtesy only when our needs for food, clothing, and shelter are met. Human beings have a great, beautiful nature, but it is difficult for this nature to fully manifest itself and bloom in our current system, which makes people struggle for survival and drives them to compete with one another. The Three Principles of Equality create the social conditions for everyone to head toward a civilization of coexistence, realizing their existential value and pursuing completion.

The Future of the Nation-State and the New Global Community

In September 2017, a newly emerging nation with a previously unheard-of name, "Asgardia," launched an artificial satellite. This feat was a remarkable achievement for a newly emerging nation, but even more surprising was that the country has no real territory on the planet. Nevertheless, currently, about one million people are reportedly registered as citizens. Asgardia is a virtual nation standing for peaceful space development advocated by Igor Ashurbeyli, the founder of the Aerospace International Research Center in Vienna, Austria.

Bitnation is another virtual, alternative country. Created in 2014 by Susanne Tarkowski Tempelhof, a former Swedish hacker, this country was designed by applying the smart-contract technology of Ethereum, a blockchain-based virtual currency. The nature of blockchain technology prevents anyone from monopolizing or controlling information and allows the implementation of direct democracy, with everyone participating in decision-making.

Even if they don't take the form of a country, many communities with a direct democratic decision-making structure based on blockchain technology are emerging in the digital space centered on shared values and visions. One example is a Decentralized Autonomous Organization (DAO), a self-governing organization managed by computer codes and programs. People who voluntarily gather for a specific purpose use blockchain technology to do their work without central authorities, regulations, or conflicts between organizations or projects.

We may take the concept of the nation-state for granted, but the modern nation-state was born out of the civil revolutions of the eighteenth century. Most key institutions that make up the state as we know it—such as the rule of law, citizenship, and representation—are recent social inventions. It's easy to think that race, ideology, religion, and culture determine the world's political dynamics. But in fact, one of the most fundamental factors is geographic location. Even if your political ideologies or religious beliefs differ from someone else's, you don't need to be hostile if you're far removed from them. When you're geographically close, however, you may be perceived as a threat to each other. But

The Art of Coexistence

if people form countries based on their own choices, values, and vision, regardless of distance, the current concept of "geopolitics" becomes meaningless. Once existing only in the imagination, such possibilities are now becoming a reality. The virtual nation is one such example.

The virtual nation allows us to experiment—by using technologies like virtual reality, the metaverse, and blockchain in an integrated way—with alternative worlds we can imagine but can't create in reality. It opens opportunities for us to attempt to create ideal countries, implementing innovative welfare institutions such as direct democracy and the equal distribution of basic income. By applying, in reality, the experiences, insights, and social consensus gained through such attempts, we can make actual countries closer to virtual ones.

If life and business in a virtual nation outgrow real space, the virtual-space community may replace the real-space community. The geopolitical concept of the nation-state and nationality based on where a person just happened to be born may become obsolete. After a virtual nation is fully established in digital space, its members may even form a community in real space if they so desire.

The best outcome is probably a community in which all people participate as real owners, based on shared values and goals being realized across the real world of Earth rather than in cyberspace. Artificially created boundaries will become meaningless, and a genuine global village will be born.

Startling new possibilities have opened before us. We can turn such prospects into reality by accepting Earth as our central value and choosing coexistence and the good of all by following the guidance of the conscience and empathy living in our hearts. Gathering our warm hearts and bright wisdom, we can create a world where the ideal of welfare is a reality, and everyone is happy. Then our planet Earth will become a great example of inspiration and innovation worthy of being benchmarked by other civilizations in the galaxy and even in other galaxies.

CHAPTER 12

Living Coexistence

"Unless someone like you cares a whole awful lot, nothing is going to get better. It's not."

— Dr. Seuss

What does it look like to incorporate the practice of coexistence into everyday life? What changes do I need to make to live as an Earth Citizen? Questions like these might make you feel that you have to do something big, or what you need to do might seem vague. But living a life helpful to yourself, others, and the planet alike is easier and more straightforward than you may think.

The first step is to recognize that you have a bright and open mind with hopes not only for your own interests but also for the health and happiness of the earth and all life. Cherish that mind. The fact that we're able to have this kind of mind is what can give humankind greatness. This is the mind of the saint and the mind of God within us.

Anyone can express this mind, but recognizing it once does not mean you are always maintaining it. This mind is not a memory; it exists in each and every moment. You need to find this mind in each moment of every day.

Anytime and anywhere, you can have a mind that wishes everyone well and thinks of the earth. However, I suggest that you take the time at least once a day to connect deeply with that mind and reconfirm its presence. I start my day by getting up early in the morning and meditating. To me, meditation is a time to make my mind pure once again. I put the goals and dreams I cherish into that bright, pure mind, and then I pray with sincere devotion. In my meditation and prayer, I visualize a healthy and beautiful earth and see countless people making changes to better themselves and the world. Also, I find new ideas and energy for working toward harmonious coexistence through early morning meditation.

Meeting with your mind doesn't necessarily mean that you have to close your eyes and sit in meditation. Every person will have their own process that feels most suitable for them. For some, that might be journaling or reflecting on the day over a cup of tea. It could be opening up and sharing your heart in conversation with someone you're close to or having a lively discussion. Whatever form it takes, include time in your day to reflect on your experiences and connect with the mindset of coexistence inside yourself.

The mindset of coexistence is a way to help ourselves before we can benefit other people and the earth. This frame of mind heals our body, develops the brain's latent potential, and gifts us with inspiration and energy. It also provides us with the wisdom to make better choices. Expressing it is a way to recover nature within ourselves, too. The mindset of coexistence is in no way complicated or burdensome but a way to be healthier, happier, and more peaceful. When nature inside us is restored, it manifests as natural healing, sensibility toward the earth and the environment, and empathy toward the people and other life forms around us.

Hope is the most incredible and beautiful thing the mind can create. Sustainable living and a world of coexistence are not beyond our reach. It starts with a sincere desire for coexistence, a goal to create a sustainable world for everyone, and the hope that this is possible. We need only have that hope and begin with whatever small thing we can do.

We can do many things to create a healthy lifestyle, and it's easy to choose a small goal that's helpful to the earth and serves harmonious coexistence. I recommend you start with what's simple and easy, something you can do right away. The specifics can vary depending on your immediate environment, lifestyle, or interests. I'm suggesting five directions that will be personally helpful for you and also good for the earth.

Keeping the Earth in Mind as We Choose Coexistence

As I have mentioned several times in this book, we're living in an era when we can directly affect the earth's future with our individual choices. Every one of our actions makes a big difference.

Let's remember the earth in every choice and action, from simple things like grocery purchases and the mode of transportation we take to social media and elections. Let's determine what is helpful to the earth, and even if that turns out to be something that's a little inconvenient personally, let's make the choices that are good for the planet. Let's remember the simple and obvious truth that what's good for others and good for the earth is ultimately the best thing for ourselves.

There are many ways to be proactive in your daily life. Examples include protecting our health through natural methods, not using disposable products, conserving water and energy, using objects with care so you can reuse them, reducing consumption of meat and increasing consumption of vegetables produced locally, reducing screen time and increasing face-to-face interaction, and finding and sharing good news to give hope and strength to one another. These aren't things you have to learn anew to put into practice; just exercise a little more conscience with what you're already doing. And these things don't require self-sacrifice but benefit you directly. At the same time, they help others and also help the earth.

Let's choose coexistence in every relationship. If you experience conflict or discord in your life, rather than accepting that as inevitable, take a breath and respond with openness and curiosity. Ask what you could do that would be helpful for everyone. Instead of trying to shrewdly find a way to win others over to your viewpoint, seek the wisdom to find the way of coexistence. The light that will show you the path of coexistence is already inside you. Ask your heart and follow the guidance of your conscience and empathy. Every time you do that, your mind will open and become brighter.

Communicating and Connecting

Many people around us—including others reading this—are not only concerned about the future of the earth and humankind but also feel a sense of responsibility. People concerned about the earth's continued existence who want to protect it need to connect and bring their strengths together. There has never been a time in human history when solidarity among people sharing a cause has been more urgent than it is now. All the communication technologies we now have, including various social media, provide a powerful means of making this kind of solidarity possible.

While all the choices and actions we make as individuals have an impact, when we are connected, that power becomes amplified into something much more significant. A wave that starts with a single message, action, and voice can produce huge ripples that spread across the world. Rather than staying in a comfort zone of feeling and knowing that there are people who share the same mind and have the same thoughts as we do, we can take a step forward and reach out our hands. We have to affirm the other person's existence and let them know of our existence.

Nothing connects people more deeply than sharing the same worries and hopes, especially when those hopes go beyond our personal interests to serve the whole. That's what partnership is about—what it means to be on the same team. When we are connected, our actions become encouragement for each other, the information we share gives us strength, and good news inspires us.

Concern and hope for the world's future apply to everyone, so no one should be left out of this connection.

Lack of knowledge or skills can no longer be an excuse. Being older or younger is no reason for exemption. Inadequate governmental policies or societal systems are not an acceptable justification. No matter where you live or what you do, whatever your skin color or religious tradition, nothing should be an obstacle. Let's share our concerns and hopes about our precious earth through all the channels of communication we now have, both online and off. Let's cheer each other on and keep developing our network. This interconnectedness creates real power for changing the world.

Practicing Natural Health

Many believe medicine, doctors, or hospitals "fix" illness. This idea has become so firmly established as "common sense" that being the proponent of an opposing view would sound strange. However, every medical tradition in the world uses the natural healing mechanisms in the body. Our bodies have self-diagnosis, auto-recovery, and regeneration mechanisms, always ready to work to restore balance when needed. Medical treatments such as drugs, physical therapy, and surgery ultimately demonstrate effectiveness because the internal natural healing mechanisms work.

Our dependence on high-cost healthcare systems centered on advanced equipment, specialists, and drug prescriptions make our lives vulnerable. It is often impossible for people without the sufficient economic capacity to get help from these healthcare systems. On the other hand, if each individual could naturally maintain their health, both individuals and society would have greater adaptability and resilience. The total cost to society could be reduced, and those financial resources could be used to make our lives more stable and sustainable in the long run, such as for improving infrastructure and the environment.

The increased use of drugs has also become a factor in environmental pollution. Disposal of pharmaceutical products—particularly those included in the general waste of homes that end up in landfills or are dumped into the sewer system—contributes significantly to soil and water pollution. Reducing the use of pharmaceutical products can help reduce water and soil pollution.

Health needn't be achieved with difficulty through artificial means. Health is a right granted to all life by nature and is the most natural state of life. When we recover and maintain our health simply and naturally, it doesn't only help save the energy and resources used to maintain health and treat diseases. It could lead to overall changes in human lifestyles and enhance the earth's natural healing power.

The following are three practical ways to improve your health naturally. Anyone can do these, and they will be helpful no matter who you are.

Breathe Well

Because we breathe as long as we're alive, it's easy to take breathing for granted. But breathing is a master key that regulates the stress response, restoring the balance of the autonomic nervous system and allowing natural healing power to perform its function. As part of the autonomic nervous system, the sympathetic nerves create the stress response when activated, and the parasympathetic nerves induce the relaxation response.

"Fight or flight" stress responses that help people respond to a crisis were originally thought to be activated only when necessary. But in modern society, we constantly make crisis situations for ourselves with negative information and thoughts that activate sympathetic nerves. In this situation, the parasympathetic nerves—which regulate digestion, rest, and recovery—are suppressed, so the body cannot exert its natural healing power. Prolonged stress is known to be the cause of most chronic diseases. As originally intended by nature, the parasympathetic nerves are activated most of the time, while the sympathetic nerves are activated only when necessary. But this balance has become reversed in many people.

Breathing is the simplest, most powerful way to calm the sympathetic nerves and restore activation of the parasympathetic nerves. Simply taking three or four deep, comfortable breaths can immediately correct the balance between these systems. There is no particular way you need to breathe, and you don't have to schedule a specific time for this. You can do it whenever stress builds up or when your head feels hot and your chest tight. There exists inside us a powerful system that helps with natural healing. By breathing, you can help this system demonstrate its power.

More specifically, try inhaling three times and then exhaling three times when you breathe. Usually, the amount of air we inhale is a small part of our lung capacity. You might think you've inhaled enough with a single breath, but you can then breathe in some more, and from there, you can breathe in even more. By inhaling three times in succession, you can quickly circulate air throughout your entire body while using your lungs as much as possible, and you can make your head clear by supplying a lot of oxygen to your brain. The same process applies to exhaling. The air in the lungs does not completely exchange when you usually exhale. So when you think you're done exhaling, breathe out again, and then breathe out one more time. The lungs will be completely emptied and can be refilled with fresh air.

Breathe in one, two, and three times with the feeling of filling up your lungs with air, and then pause for a moment to focus on the feeling of your chest expanding. When you exhale, breathe out as if you are dividing the air into three portions to release all the air in your lungs. Feel a satisfying sense of fullness when you breathe in and a lighter, refreshed sensation when you breathe out. Even five to 10 repetitions will make your brain waves drop, and your mind will become calm. When you find yourself in stressful situations in your daily life, this can calm your mind quickly.

Take Care of Your Gut

The gut is more than just part of the digestive system. It has a neural network with about 300 to 500 million nerve cells—the body's second-largest neural network after the brain. That's why the gut is called the "second brain."

Among the main hormones in our bodies, serotonin makes us feel pleasure, and dopamine gives us a sense of reward. The gut is where 50 percent of the dopamine and 95 percent of the serotonin in our body is produced. In other words, the pleasure and happiness we feel are determined more by the condition of our gut than by our brain.

The gut accounts for 80 percent of our body's immune system. Microbes living in the gut take on that role; the number of microbes in the gut is about 10 times more than the number of cells in our body. The condition of these tiny tenants affects our immune system and our brain. An effective way to help these gut microbes healthily do their job is to eat fermented foods, such as kimchi, natto (fermented soybeans), and sauerkraut.

It's also a good idea to do exercises stimulating the gut, including abdominal tapping, intestinal exercise, and abdominal massage. These exercises effectively increase core temperature, which is known to be closely related to natural immunity.

Abdominal tapping involves clapping rhythmically on the lower abdomen with the palms of both hands or tapping with the hands held lightly in fists. To do intestinal exercises, you repeatedly pull the lower belly inward as much as possible and then release it. You may find intestinal exercises a bit difficult at first because you're not used to moving your abdominal muscles that way, but with practice, you can quickly get the hang of it. Start with about 20 to 30 reps, increasing that number bit by bit so that you can do about 100 repetitions at a time. Repeat sets of 100 in succession as many times as you can. For abdominal massage, you press into your belly with the fingertips of your hands together or rub your palms over your belly gently.

Utilizing a combination of abdominal tapping, intestinal exercise, and abdominal massage activates the gut and increases the temperature of the lower abdomen, improving immunity as well as increasing resistance to stress.

Eat Smaller Portions, Mindfully

Improving dietary habits is one of the most effective ways of enhancing natural health *and* responding to climate change. For example, creating pastures for cattle is the most significant cause of rainforest destruction. Methane gas produced by cows and carbon dioxide have been identified as major factors in climate change. That's why improving the way you eat can be helpful for your own health and the earth as a whole.

No one diet is right for everyone. You need to find the food that's good for you according to your own constitution, body type, and state of health. However, nutritionists' guidelines tell us what's good for individuals and the earth. We need to reduce our consumption of meat—especially red meat such as beef—and eat more vegetables, especially those that contain a lot of natural fiber. (Of course, organic and locally farmed vegetables are even better.) Eating lots of veggies helps you eliminate toxins from the body, stabilize your blood sugar, and maintain a proper weight. It also reduces energy consumed for transportation, preserves natural forests, and helps prevent soil and water pollution. This change is simple but surprisingly helpful.

Eating smaller portions of food is also helpful. While anorexia is a real problem, especially in first-world countries, being overweight or obese has become so prevalent that medical experts now classify it as a pandemic. There are many reasons for the increased rate of obesity, which causes many diseases in countries around the world, but the biggest one is that binge eating and overeating have become a part of everyday life. *What* you eat is important, but the real problem is *how much* you eat. We are simply eating way too much. No matter how good something may be for your body—for example, organic vegetables with brown rice—overeating is poisonous.

Eating as a meditative practice can be one way to prevent overeating. Simply put, this involves focusing on what you feel in your body as you eat. While you eat, feel the sensations of chewing, the taste, the feeling of food moving through your esophagus, and so on. This way, the feeling of eating becomes richer, and you experience much deeper pleasure than what you would feel at the tip of your tongue. Focus on your body's responses as you eat, and stop when your body tells you you've had enough. If you eat anymore, it's not your body doing the eating, but your taste buds and habits.

There's no measurable index for overeating. The amount to consume depends on the person, and it'll be different for the same person at different times depending on their condition. To set the simplest and most natural standard, anything you eat beyond what your body needs right now counts as overeating. That's why it's so important to feel your body and listen to its signals. That is the most natural way to control your diet.

One thing to remember is to eat thankfully and happily. If it feels burdensome and stressful to pick out healthy food, then it's no better than not making an effort. Regardless of what food you choose, don't add toxins from your mind with negative emotions. Eat that food with joy, thanking every being that made sacrifices and contributions so that it could be in front of you.

The ways to practice natural health introduced here are things anyone can do alone. They don't have to be learned from an expert, and you don't have to wait for changes in policy or the healthcare system. These are things you can do right now if you choose to.

These small actions not only solve personal problems, such as being overweight, but they are the key to creating a peaceful and sustainable world. They can lead us to make different choices in our daily lives and bring about changes in politics, the economy, and industry. Sharing the experiences of natural health and natural healing with those around you also improves the larger communities' health and promotes harmony with the environment.

Simplify Your Life and Eliminate Waste

Do you know how much "stuff" you own? If you're like most people, it probably numbers in the thousands—or more. How many of those items are you currently using? How many things have you not even touched in the past year or two? If you haven't used something for a year, it's probably unlikely that you'll use it in the future.

Two examples of waste most closely related to our daily lives are clothing and food. Of all the clothes produced,

30 percent don't sell and end up being discarded. Most so-called luxury brands are known to burn and dispose of unsold clothing rather than sell it at low prices to maintain their brand value. Even clothes people purchase are often discarded after being used for a brief time due to short-term fashion trends. Because clothing has a low recycling rate due to the nature of the materials, more than 85 percent of discarded clothing goes to incinerators or landfills.

The same applies to food. In the United States, for example, 40 percent of food ingredients and products, including fruits, vegetables, meat, and processed foods, are thrown away without being used. The statistics for the whole world are also high—33 percent. The vast amounts of water, electricity, labor, and government subsidies that went into producing these foods are being discarded as well. And as foods decompose in landfills, a massive amount of methane is released into the atmosphere, and pollutants enter the soil and drinking water sources.

Furthermore, not everything that ends up in the hands of consumers gets eaten; 50 to 60 percent of the world's food waste consists of leftovers. Simply put, we produce about three times what the world's population can consume, and more than a third of that gets discarded before being used. Of what remains, half is eaten, and half is thrown away.

This wasteful production and consumption pattern especially applies to clothing and food, but it's happening in every area of our lives, from personal electronic devices such as mobile phones to cars and houses. And it doesn't just end with waste; it makes the earth and the life within us sick. Every day, the plastic waste we throw away gets buried in the ground or flows into the oceans. Right now, there is an island of garbage in the middle of the Pacific Ocean that is twice the size of Texas or three times the size of France. Microplastics leach out of this trash and cycle through the marine ecosystem, going around and around until they eventually enter our bodies.

Every object has its purpose and value. We can realize that value by respecting and using things properly. If we cannot do that, we can let people who can use those objects do so. We usually don't think about recycling until it's time to throw something away, deciding whether to put it in a regular trash can or a recycling bin. By sharing something with others, we can start recycling it much earlier, when it still has value. We can shift from inconsiderate and wasteful consumption to kind, thoughtful, and sustainable use by using and sharing things mindfully.

We don't necessarily need new technologies or systems to actualize sustainability. Nor do we have to scale down our lives and give up the conveniences we currently enjoy. By eliminating wastefulness, we can improve our quality of life and reduce the stress burdening our own lives and the earth. When you simplify your life and reduce unnecessary things, you get more breathing room in your life—as well as the mental space for new creation.

Being Kind

Larry King once asked the Dalai Lama to appear on his talk show. One of the questions King asked him was, "What is compassion?" Since that's a core tenet of Buddhism, many people would have expected the Dalai Lama to come up with some grand and profound explanation. But his answer was unexpectedly simple. The Dalai Lama said, "It's being kind." This simple, straightforward answer inspires a happy smile. Practicing coexistence doesn't require tremendous self-sacrifice or commitment. It's expressed sufficiently with a bit of kindness.

If you feel that the world isn't all that kind, try jogging your memory a bit. When you've gone in and out of a building, have there been more people who let the door slam back in your face or more who held it open for you? There were likely incomparably more who held the door for you. There is an overwhelming amount of kindness in the world. Unkindness from a lack of consideration is rare, and intentional cruelty is rarer still. Through the power of kindness, life is bearable, and society is maintained. Kindness comes from the original nature of empathy and compassion within us. That's why it's much easier to be kind than unkind.

Even without exerting great effort, we can practice kindness toward ourselves and others, the animals and plants around us, and even the objects we use. If we cherish and use the objects around us, large and small, with care and without rough and abusive handling, we can use them for a longer time without their breaking down. This habit is helpful to you and the earth. The great and small kindnesses we can carry out without investing huge effort make our lives safer and the earth more sustainable.

We might think the earth is so big that changing it is beyond our ability. But in fact, we are already doing that. Currently, the most influential force on the earth's systems is us. By using our power more carefully and wisely, we can create a sustainable world of coexistence for everyone. Let's keep the earth in mind and choose coexistence in all areas and relationships of life. Let's feel a sense of responsibility for the earth's future and humankind and communicate and connect with people who create new hope. Let's become healthier through natural methods, eliminate waste, and treat ourselves and the people and things around us with a little more kindness. Even small actions can make significant changes possible.

Such practices are helpful first for yourself. Your relationships are expanded, there's more breathing room in your life, stress is reduced, and time and energy can be used efficiently. We can make our lives and the communities to which we belong healthier and more abundant. Moreover, we can create a world where the actual value of coexistence is realized—a healthy, harmonious, and sustainable community of life consisting of the earth and all the creatures living on it. This possibility is open to us. We can make it happen.

Choosing Hope with All Our Might

This book is my cover letter, action plan, and an invitation to partners and compatriots. Through it, I've expressed the hopes and fears I have for the future of the earth and the dreams I want to achieve for the earth and humankind. I've also shared the activities I've participated in until now because I want to connect, communicate, and act together with other people who have in their hearts the same love, hope, and concern for the earth that I do. I'm looking for people who have the eagerness that makes us willing to give it a try, whatever it takes. That desire forms the beginning and end of this book.

Forty years ago, I saw two images of Earth at the end of a meditation exercise to find my purpose in life. One was a beautiful and healthy Earth where humans and nature lived harmoniously. The other version of Earth was destroyed and devastated, where all life, including humans, was dying in unspeakable pain. Though marked by such contrast, these two aspects of Earth were as close as the two sides of a single coin. Since then, I have lived with one goal, devoting my life to making the earth look like the first version I saw in my meditation.

Everyone needs something to live for and to motivate them to face life's difficulties. That something would naturally make you so focused on it that you could think of nothing else. For some people, the object of this unwavering, single-minded focus could be a loved one, their chosen life purpose, or the religious conviction to which they dedicate themselves.

For me, it is a world of harmonious coexistence, with humankind at peace and a healthy Earth. If a task helps reach this goal, it has become infused into my very being to jump into it without hesitation, even if I'm utterly inexperienced and others are gravely concerned that I'll fail. I have been working without asking whether something will succeed or fail. Instead, I ask whether or not it is necessary for a world of coexistence.

Sometimes, putting everything on the line to jump into something opened the door for something even bigger and connected me with even more people. That was how I went from sharing Dahnhak in South Korea to moving my base of activity to the United States and introducing these Korean mind-body training methods to the world. I established Brain Education as an academic discipline and founded the Global Cyber University to cultivate Earth Citizens. By a stroke of good fortune, it became the alma mater of most of the members of BTS, a record-breaking, K-pop boy band that became a global phenomenon. The meditation center I developed in the wilderness of Sedona, Arizona, in the US inspires the thousands of people who visit yearly.

I always harbor a deep yearning for a healthy human race and Earth, so whomever I'd meet or whatever I'd see or hear would become connected with this goal—and that would start something new. As one part of this journey, something I've come to focus on lately is flavor and herbs. I've been interested in herbs for natural health for a long time, and I've been studying them steadily for a while. Among them is one in particular that recently attracted my special attention.

The Power of Bitter Taste

As the pandemic was winding down, I returned to Sedona, Arizona, which is the home of the Earth Citizen Movement to me. Whenever I come to Sedona, I make it part of my day to hike on the many trails surrounding this small city.

One day, as I walked along between the beautiful, red rocks and the lush, green juniper forests, a plant standing in a grove of trees suddenly caught my eye. It seemed to glow with a silvery light so clear and intense that, although I passed the tree and continued for a while, I soon returned as though drawn to it.

The tree was covered in teardrop-shaped, green-gray leaves. I picked a leaf, closely examined its shape, and smelled its fragrance. I felt the urge to taste the leaf, so I tore off a tiny piece about the size of a grain of rice, put it in my mouth, and gave it a chew. Even though the piece of leaf was so small, it created a sensory explosion in my mouth. It was so shockingly and intensely bitter that it put an uncontrollable grimace on my face and caused saliva to pool rapidly in my mouth. But I didn't hate it. It was intense but not lingering. As I continued to hold the leaf in my mouth, the flavor neutralized into a clean, subtle bitter flavor. My brain and body felt clear and fresh like I had just taken a deep breath of crisp air.

I steadied my breathing and quietly focused on the sensations I felt, and behind the bitter taste, I sensed a subtly sweet flavor as my body and mind became calm and comfortable. I experienced my energy being balanced, bringing cool energy to my head and warm energy to my lower belly. I felt love and blessings from nature and every life form. In a moment of inspiration, I strongly sensed that these leaves could greatly help people. I gave this herb the name "coexistence plant" on the spot. I later learned that the herb is known by many names, most commonly "silk tassel," but I like to call it coexistence plant because of what it means to me.

I picked a few leaves of the plant and went back home. It was then I discovered that the house I'd been living in for 20 years had the same tree growing in the backyard. It had always been there, and I simply hadn't noticed it. This experience is how my meeting with the coexistence plant came about. It would be more accurate to say that it found me rather than I found it.

Although the coexistence plant was close, because I had been unaware of it, I couldn't use it. Even if there's something unique and precious right in front of your nose, if you don't know that it exists, it's as if it's not there. The sense of coexistence is no different. Although the sense of harmonious coexistence has always been inside us, if we don't realize it or think of it as important and give it value, and if we don't use that sense in our everyday lives, it's the same as not having it at all.

Right now, I'm struck by the charm of this herb. I've steeped it into a tea to drink, made a balm out of it to use on the skin, and developed different recipes to put it in the food I eat. To help more people experience its bitter taste, I've balanced it with sweetness and made a form of hard candy. It seems that the coexistence plant lends itself well to broad usage for natural health, so I've also started to research it in earnest with a specialized team.

Strange as it may sound, the appeal of this herb lies in its unique bitter flavor. There is a saying that "Good medicine is bitter." When it comes to bitterness, you could probably say that this herb is the ultimate "good medicine"—it's that bitter. It is bitter in the mouth but better for the body.

Many people tend to avoid bitter flavors, especially children. As we get older, we start to like bitter flavors more, such as black coffee or dark chocolate. That's the way it should be, since you need more of the invigorating bitter flavor as you age to keep you youthful and energetic. But, unfortunately, modern people have become far too addicted to sweet flavors, and most of us eat far too much sugar and other sweeteners. Even many savory processed foods have added corn syrup and such. This is bad for our bodies, leading to conditions like obesity and diabetes, and it is an indication that taste-wise, we are remaining in an immature, childlike state.

Bitter flavor is not just bitter. If you hold the bitter taste in your mouth for a long time, sweet saliva pools in your mouth. This is the response to bitter taste that the brain produces through the body. It's similar to how, when you stimulate the tongue's pain trigger points with a spicy taste, the brain releases endorphins and makes you feel pleasure. Although the brain reacts passively to sweet flavors, it responds actively to bitter flavors, making changes of its own accord. The bitter taste wakes up the brain and makes it move creatively.

The sweet flavor may be pleasant in the mouth, but it causes many health problems. In particular, it makes the blood stale and causes obesity, diabetes, high blood pressure, and inflammation. The bitter taste has the opposite effect, helping to suppress and alleviate obesity, diabetes, high blood pressure, and inflammation. It is known in Eastern medicine that the bitter taste makes the mind clear, aids digestion, and reduces heat in the heart, allowing the mind to find calm and enhancing the body's immune response.

The autonomic nerves are responsible for harmony and balance in our bodies. The balance between sympathetic and parasympathetic nerves in many people is disrupted right now. Amid unlimited competition, there is constant tension, anxiety, and excitement, and the sympathetic nerves are overly active. In contrast, the function of the parasympathetic nerves, which brings relaxation and calms the mind, is suppressed. The suppressed parasympathetic nerves need to be revived.

Such a revival is already known to be achieved by practices such as breathing and meditation, which I have been teaching for many years to help people recover their health and well-being. They also create proper energy balance within the body's energy system, a state called "Water Up, Fire Down." In that state, the head remains cool and calm, while heat energy pools in the lower abdomen.

Recently, I had been looking for ways to use the senses of taste and smell to support these experiences, which I suppose is why I felt drawn to the coexistence plant. This herb with an intense bitter taste was a wonderful discovery since the brain automatically responds to the plant's properties, reversing the body's sympathetic stress response and balancing the body's energy. Thus through effortless sensing of flavor and fragrance, people who may have trouble meditating or focusing can find it easier to calm their minds and allow respite for their bodies for self-care and self-healing. Studying the coexistence plant is the beginning of such an attempt.

It's difficult to change habits of addiction through gradual changes. It's hard to stop smoking cigarettes by cutting them down by one each day; you have to stop all at once. One effective way to change a palate accustomed to sweet flavors isn't to reduce sweet tastes gradually but to stimulate the brain with bitter flavors and develop a taste for bitter things. In doing so, you can recalibrate your palate, control your weight, and improve your health. Bitter flavor is the taste of coexistence that corrects the balance of the brain and restores the physiological balance of our body. I have high hopes that the coexistence plant can be helpful for finding harmony and balance between mind and body.

I believe this rush of bitter flavor effectively unclogs and cleans the entire energy system, almost like an energetic roto-rooter. Because of our overly competitive lifestyle and lack of mindfulness culture, many of us have habitually imbalanced energy systems, and we are carrying imbalanced energy from past life experiences. In addition to practices like breathing and meditation, we can use herbs like the coexistence plant to start healing ourselves from the energetic level.

I am only beginning to research the coexistence plant and bitter flavors. After more time has passed, there will likely be many stories that I can share with you. One thing is certain: all the experiences, learning, and insight I will gain from the coexistence plant, just like all of the other experiences of my life, will be used in my vision of realizing a peaceful human race and a healthy Earth. I am focusing on this vision day and night with unforgettable longing and unwavering, single-minded focus.

If there is a goal that we really want, and we are always focused on that goal and stay open-minded, we can discover many new opportunities around us. In a sense, every encounter you have is an opportunity, and every person is a supporter. Amid such opportunities and encounters, you can achieve your goal. I hope that my coexistence plant story gives you that kind of inspiration. And I hope that *your* experience, *your* story, and the insights you've attained will contribute to saving the central value of the earth that we all share.

A Reason for Hope

These days, every day, I feel more desperately and clearly the meaning of that vision, the two versions of Earth that I saw 40 years ago. The two conflicting possibilities now exist simultaneously like two multiverses. Big or small, every thought we have, every choice we make, and every action we take keeps shifting the direction of the world we're living in toward one possibility or another. My mind also lurches back and forth between worry and hope. I think that many people feel this way now.

I choose hope with all my might in that jostle between worry and hope. The object of my hope, the strength that makes me have hope, is neither prophecy nor God. It's not even the beautiful version of Earth I saw 40 years ago. What gives me hope is the beautiful and good heart inside me and you that worries for the future of the earth and humankind and desperately wants everything to work out well for everyone. Worry and hope come from the same mind. I choose hope because that is the only choice to make in the end.

I want to tell the readers of this book that every one of us should have a profound respect for ourselves. We are by no means small. In our brains, each of us has a mind shining with infinite potential, creativity, and the essential nature of harmonious coexistence. We can change our lives and save ourselves and the earth by finding and using that mind.

With this book, I would like to express my gratitude to the countless people who have participated in the Earth Citizen Movement over the years. They are the greatest blessings of my life and have kept me holding on to my hopes and dreams and faith in human beings and the world. And I am deeply grateful to you for reading this book to the end. I hope you will do what you can for harmonious coexistence so that we can all thrive together, following the sincere voice and feeling that arises in your heart. I hope we can meet someday on the path of practicing harmonious coexistence. I want to meet you, who are wiser and have greater passion than I do, and work together with you for a peaceful, sustainable earth.

Acknowledgments

I've been speaking about and teaching the core concepts in this book for a long time, but it was finally time to synthesize them into a publication designed for the current age. I couldn't have done this without Steve Kim, my long-time student and vision partner who helped create a flow of ideas and added details that gave the concepts new life.

I also appreciate Daniel Graham and Eunyoung Seo, who masterfully translated the Korean manuscript into English, and Nicole Dean and Phyllis Elving for their artful, expert editing. Kiryl Lysenka, who has designed many of my books, brought a new depth to this one, and I thank him for his efforts on the cover and interior.

This book could never have been made without the staff at my US publisher, Best Life Media. Thank you once again. Finally, to all the people I've met and to the Brain Education practitioners around the globe, I'm thankful to have learned so much from you and to have witnessed your passion for a harmonious and peaceful world.

About the Authors

Ilchi Lee is an author, educator, and humanitarian who has devoted his life to teaching energy principles and developing methods to nurture the full potential of the human brain.

For the last four decades, his mission has been to help people harness their creative power. For this goal, he developed mind-body training methods such as Body & Brain Yoga and Brain Education, which have inspired many people worldwide to live healthier and happier lives. He also founded the undergraduate Global Cyber University and the graduate University of Brain Education.

Lee has penned more than 40 books, including the *New York Times* bestseller *The Call of Sedona: Journey of the Heart*, as well as *The Power Brain: Five Steps to Upgrading Your Brain Operating System* and *I've Decided to Live 120 Years: The Ancient Secret to Longevity, Vitality, and Life Transformation*.

A well-respected humanitarian, Ilchi Lee has worked with the United Nations and other organizations for global peace through his nonprofit International Brain Education Association (IBREA Foundation). In addition, he began the Earth Citizen Movement, a global drive to raise awareness of the value of living mindfully and sustainably as a steward of the earth, and started the nonprofit Earth Citizens Organization (ECO). For more information about Ilchi Lee, visit Ilchi.com.

Steve Kim is a writer, educator, and life-long practitioner of mindfulness and sustainable living. He is one Ilchi Lee's closest students and has worked with him as a vision partner for Ilchi Lee's educational and sociocultural endeavors.

In 1997, he helped establish Tao Fellowship as an organization that promotes the spirit of Tao as universal principles for peace and harmony. He served the organization as its president for 10 years.

Steve Kim also helped establish the Earth Citizens Organization (ECO) in 2014, a nonprofit dedicated to promoting mindful living, natural health, and world sustainability. He currently serves ECO as its executive director.

Resources

Ilchi Lee's Email Newsletter

Ilchi Lee sends weekly inspirational messages, tips, and meditations on how to live a life of coexistence and fulfillment. Get ongoing advice and encouragement for connecting with your heart and mind and using them to create a bright future. Sign up at Ilchi.com/newsletter.

Earth Citizens Organization (ECO)

This nonprofit founded by Ilchi Lee and run by Steve Kim promotes mindful living and natural health for a sustainable world. It provides leadership programs that develop individuals' skills and strengths to foster an Earth Citizen lifestyle in communities. It also runs the ECO Farm, which offers programs that deliver practical skills that connect food and wellness. To learn more, visit EarthCitizens.org

Body & Brain Yoga and Tai Chi Classes

Find classes with expert instructors in yoga, tai chi, and meditation at Body & Brain Yoga Tai Chi centers. There are about 100 centers across the United States, with more in South Korea, Japan, Europe, Canada, and New Zealand. Group classes, workshops, and individual sessions are available both online and offline. Find a US center near you at BodynBrain.com.

Books of Related Interest

The following books can also help you practice harmonious coexistence and the Earth Citizen lifestyle. See them all and more of Ilchi Lee's books at BestLifeMedia.com.

Change
Realizing Your Greatest Potential

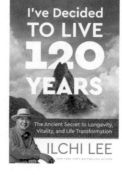

I've Decided to Live 120 Years
The Ancient Secret to Longevity, Vitality, and Life Transformation

Earth Management
A Dialogue on Ancient Korean Wisdom and Its Lessons for a New Earth

Living Tao
Timeless Principles for Everyday Enlightenment

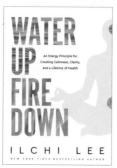

Water Up Fire Down
An Energy Principle for Creating Calmness, Clarity, and a Lifetime of Health

The Power Brain
Five Steps to Upgrading Your Brain Operating System